THE OFFICIAL MOVIE BOOK
JODY DUNCAN

ACKNOWLEDGMENTS

Yabba Dabba Doos to MCA's Nancy Crushing-Bones and Jennifer SeaBreeze for giving me the opportunity to tell the behind-the-scenes story of another fascinating Univershell/Amblin production. Thanks to Dave Cunningstone, Nick Rocktinez and Slabrielle Smith for backstage creativity; to John Shanrock for comedic input; and to Don and Estelle Shale, Gem Hatch and Janine Pourrock for encouragement and support.

My gratitude is also extended to all the production and creative personnel from *The Flintstones* who took precious time out of hectic schedules to talk with me – some on the telephone, some from across the Atlantic, some in the comfort of their own homes. I am especially indebted to Hollyrock dynamos Brian Levant and Bruce Cohen, whose schedules were the most hectic of all, but who both gave graciously and generously of their time and insight.

Thanks to Billy Pigasaurus, a true partner in this project.

Hugs and kisses to my own little Pebbles doll, Caitlin, who contributed greatly by restraining herself and asking only every ten minutes or so if the book was done yet.

Finally, a huge, brontosaurus-sized thank you to Jerry 'The Rock' Schmitz of Amblin/Universal, who was truly a rock throughout the writing of this book.

Thanks, everyone. I had a gay old time!

JODY DUNCAN

Artwork/photos courtesy of:
Sven Arnstein, Tim Flattery, Peter Iovino, Marty Kline,
George Lange, Dave Lowery, Stephen F Morely, Tim Street Porter,
Alan Tinkley and Ron Batzdorff, Unit photographer

A Mandarin Paperback
The Flintstones Official Movie Book

First published in Great Britain 1994
by Mandarin Paperbacks
an imprint of Reed Consumer Books Limited
Michelin House, 81 Fulham Road, London SW3 6RB
and Auckland, Melbourne, Singapore and Toronto

A CIP catalogue record for this title
is available from the British Library

ISBN 0 7493 1922 4

Printed and bound in United Kingdom

Editor Julian Brown
Design Sue Michniewicz, Rabab Adams
Production Michelle Thomas

CONTENTS

INTRODUCTION 6

CHAPTER 1
PREPRODUCTION 8

CHAPTER 2
CASTING 16

CHAPTER 3
PRODUCTION DESIGN 26

CHAPTER 4
CREATURES 48

CHAPTER 5
SPECIAL EFFECTS 66

CHAPTER 6
THE SHOOT 76

CHAPTER 7
POSTPRODUCTION 88

CHAPTER 8
ON RELEASE 94

INTRODUCTION

The medium of television was not even fifteen years old when, on the evening of September 30, 1960, ABC premiered *The Flintstones*. Created by the highly successful Hanna-Barbera animation studio, *The Flintstones* was an altogether unique offering: the first adult cartoon, the first program-length cartoon, and the first animated situation comedy to air on primetime television. Featuring the comedic exploits of Fred Flintstone, a prehistoric Everyman and his warm but sometimes 'rocky' relationships with his wife, Wilma, and neighbors Barney and Betty Rubble, *The Flintstones* was rooted in the popular situation comedies of that era: *The Honeymooners*, most obviously, and *I Love Lucy*.

Within its classic situation comedy structure, *The Flintstones* managed to poke gentle fun at the two-cars-in-every-garage suburban mentality of American society in the early Sixties. In the quiet little town of Bedrock – located somewhere on the drifting land masses of prehistory – Fred and Barney worked hard, bowled, went to lodge meetings, and came up with one ill-conceived get-rich-quick scheme after another. Wilma and Betty kept their husbands in line, shopped, loved their children, shopped, made weekly trips to the beauty salon and, of course, shopped.

Both families enjoyed a suburban life style complete with all the modern conveniences: phonographs powered by long-beaked prehistoric birds, lobster lawnmowers, and indoor plumbing provided by genial mastodons. Wrapped in Stone Age trappings, *The Flintstones* put a mirror up to a culture that loved its 'creature comforts'. We recognized ourselves and laughed.

Clubbed by critics, *The Flintstones* was nevertheless embraced by the television audience. For six years, the show earned consistently good ratings, and eventually even swayed critical response, receiving a variety of honors, including a Golden Globe Award for outstanding achievement in international television cartoons. Despite accolades and continuing popularity, however, sponsors who were bored with the tried-and-true and eager to attach themselves to something new prompted the cancellation of the show in 1966. It was a surprising blow, not only for Hanna-Barbera, but for millions of *Flintstones* fans. *The Flintstones* would never again run as a primetime series.

And yet, Fred, Wilma, Barney and Betty have been with us ever since the show's primetime demise over thirty years ago. Not only has the original animated program appeared in syndication all over the world, countless special and Saturday morning versions of *The Flintstones* continue to be produced.

The Seventies gave us *The Flintstones Comedy Hour*, a Saturday morning serial that combined previously aired episodes with music, as well as a spin-off entitled *Pebbles and Bamm-Bamm*. Hour-long specials have included *A Flintstones Christmas*, *The Flintstones Meet Rockula and Frankenstone*, *The Flintstones Little Big League* and *The Flintstones 25th Anniversary*, a 1986 tribute hosted by Tim Conway, Harvey Korman and Vanna White. Even as recently as Fall 1993, a new Movie of the Week – *The Flintstones Hollyrock-A-Bye Baby* – aired in primetime. To this day, an estimated 300 million people continue to watch the show in eighty countries, and in twenty-two different languages.

And then there is the merchandising. The *Flintstones* characters appear regularly in comic books, on toys, lunch boxes, cereals, soap and vitamins. Such marketing tie-ins have earned the *Flintstones* worldwide recognition; and, in fact, in 1991, Mongolia issued a series of postage stamps depicting the Flintstones and Rubbles visiting the Gobi Desert. To anyone inhabiting the planet earth during the past 30 years, the Flintstones – to paraphrase John Lennon – are more well-known than the pagan gods.

Given the show's wide-ranging appeal and Gibraltar-like endurance, it seemed, an ideal vehicle for a full-length feature film. Not only were the characters an integral part of our current pop culture, they also represented a bygone era, a time when 'family values' was a subject for the family dinner table rather than fuel for a political firestorm.

A collective and nostalgic longing for that gentler era had been evidenced in Hollywood for some time. *Star Trek* has spawned six films, while two feature-length versions of *The Addams Family* have met with box-office success. *Dragnet* and *The Beverly Hillbillies* have also been translated to the big screen. And, with a *Maverick* feature in the works, the trend shows no signs of slowing. Clearly, in an attempt to lure demographically desirable baby boomers, studios were increasingly looking to the beloved television shows of the Sixties for movie-making inspiration

One such baby boomer, Steven Spielberg, first became intrigued with the idea of a *Flintstones* feature film while on the set of his 1989 movie *Always*. Cast in a supporting role in the film was John Goodman, an actor who, after years of exemplary work in movies, television and theater, had recently earned big-time stardom with his role as Dan Conner on the ABC sitcom *Roseanne*. On the *Always* set, it suddenly occurred to Spielberg that Goodman – a big man who exudes warmth, good humor and a blue-collar sensibility – was nothing less than the living, breathing incarnation of Fred Flintstone.

Unable to shake the conviction that he had stumbled upon a perfect marriage of actor and role, Spielberg approached Goodman on the first day of filming and said, 'I want you to play Fred Flintstone.' Goodman's only response was a smile.

Reaching an unofficial agreement with Goodman, Amblin Entertainment – the production company Spielberg co-founded with Kathleen Kennedy and Frank Marshall in 1984 – promptly secured the rights to the animated show from Hanna-Barbera. Enthusiasm for the project remained high at Amblin for several years, even while numerous unsuccessful attempts at a script and Goodman's limited availability kept the project on the back burner. Finally, in the summer of 1993, the movie went into production; and on May 27, 1994, *The Flintstones* opened in theaters around the country.

What has been revealed to audiences on the big screen is a more-than-faithful adaptation of the beloved cartoon show. Through a colossal production design effort, all of Bedrock was laid out in three-dimensional splendor. Through a complex special effects effort, which included animatronic puppets and computer generated characters, a host of Flintstonian critters were brought to life. And through the efforts of a talented group of actors, Fred, Barney, Wilma and Betty evolved from pen and ink drawings to live characters of flesh and bone. Driving the large-scale production was a team of young producers and a director who, quite literally, had been dreaming of making *The Flintstones* most of his life.

There are a million stories in the big city of Hollyrock. This is one of them . . .

CHAPTER 1

"FLINTSTONES, MEET THE FLINTSTONES..."

PRE-PRODUCTION

The year 1957 was the best of times and the worst of times for Bill Hanna and Joe Barbera. After twenty years at Metro-Goldwyn-Mayer – where they had produced their popular and Academy Award winning *Tom and Jerry* theatrical shorts – the animation team had been stunned when the studio suddenly and unceremoniously closed its animation department, laying off the entire staff. Requiring thousands of drawings and a like number of man-hours, the art of animation had become too costly, and MGM wanted out of the cartoon business.

Forming their own production company, Hanna and Barbera went looking for work, finally making a deal with Screen Gems to produce a six-minute animated program: *Ruff and Reddy*. But there was a catch. Rather than spend the $45,000 to $65,000 each *Tom and Jerry* short had demanded, Screen Gems was prepared to spend only $3,000 per episode of *Ruff and Reddy*. With no other offers forthcoming, Hanna-Barbera agreed. "Our backs were to the wall," Joe Barbera recalled,

opened their own studio. Hanna-Barbera's programs were so successful, in fact, that in the same year Screen Gems suggested moving animation to primetime. Polls had indicated that a surprisingly large percentage of the television cartoon audience was over eighteen years old, and Screen Gems intended to capitalize on those demographics.

Despite the polls, an animated weekly series for the whole family was, at the time, a bold idea. "No one had ever done it before," noted Barbera, "and we had no idea how to do it. So, just to give us some direction, we started looking at the situation comedies that were on at the time, including *The Honeymooners.*" What Hanna-Barbera saw in the

ABOVE: Bill Hanna, one of the creators of the original *Flintstones* cartoon, appeared in a boardroom scene in the live-action film.

"and we had to be creative: how could we do for $3,000 what we had previously done for over $50,000? Our answer was what is now known as limited animation."

Limited animation, as its name implies, required only fifteen to eighteen hundred drawings per short, as compared to the 26,000 drawings typical of a more fully-rendered cartoon. "We would use just two drawings for a run – one drawing of the feet in one position, and a second drawing of the feet in the opposing position. And then we'd switch them back and forth. We moved our camera in and out, shook the screen for hits – we used every trick in the book that we had accumulated over twenty years in the business."

Having found a way to make their work affordable once again, the animation team flourished. Enjoying success with *Ruff and Reddy*, and subsequently, *The Adventures of Huckleberry Hound* and *Quick Draw McGraw*, Hanna and Barbera were firmly established as producers of animated television programs within two years, and in 1959

popular Jackie Gleason vehicle was the classic 'two-buddies' situation that had been exemplified by Laurel and Hardy, and Abbott and Costello. "We started thinking about a show that centered on a couple of guys, putting them in a variety of situations and time periods. We came up with pilgrim buddies, and farmer buddies, and hillbilly buddies: but nothing really clicked."

Finally, someone at the studio drew up a rough sketch of a caveman and a long-beaked bird playing a phonograph record. "As soon as we saw the first rough sketch," Bill Hanna recalled, "a flood of gags came out, like the elephant with the trunk for taking a shower or watering the lawn or washing the

dishes or the car; the lizard clothespins on the line, the cars moving with the feet, a bus moving with twenty feet, that kind of thing. It just opened a world of gags."

Running with the prehistoric theme, Hanna-Barbera developed a show that was dubbed *The Flagstones*. When Hanna-Barbera was threatened with a lawsuit from the creators of *Hi and Lois*, a comic strip with characters who bore the 'Flagstone' name, the title was changed to *The Gladstones* and finally to *The Flintstones*.

Armed with 300 storyboards for two half-hour episodes, Joe Barbera went to New York and proceeded to pitch the new show to countless sponsors and network executives. "Every day I would go out and try to sell the show. I'd go over the story and act out the parts, doing all the sound effects. It took a full hour-and-a-half to go through the whole presentation. Sometimes I'd pitch it five or six times a day. Everywhere I went, people loved the idea. They'd call people in to see my pitch – 'Come see this cuckoo bird pitch this show.' But even though everybody loved it, nobody would buy it. It was just too new an idea."

On Barbera's last Friday in New York, after eight gruelling weeks, *The Flintstones* still hadn't sold. "I was flying home in an hour, but we had one pitch left, which was to ABC. So at eight-thirty that morning all the big guys from ABC came in – and they bought the show in fifteen minutes. If it hadn't sold right then, that would have been the end of it, because we were giving up and coming back home – and you don't go back the next year and pitch the same thing you had the previous year."

Sponsored by R.J. Reynolds Tobacco Company and Miles Laboratories – the company that still manufactures *Flintstones* vitamins for children – the show went into production in the spring of 1960. Allotted a budget that amounted to approximately $1,000 per minute, Hanna-Barbera again had to be creative and find a way to cut production costs. "One of our cost-savers was going to foreign countries for inking and painting," Hanna explained.

ABOVE: Joe Barbera, co-creator of the cartoon *Flintstones*, also made a cameo appearance in the live-action movie. Here he is driving his date to the Cavern on the Green nightclub for Wilma's birthday party.

"Later on we went to foreign countries for the animation as well – something which is commonplace now. Eventually, we set up a permanent operation in Australia for production. We had a key staff of animators at Hanna-Barbera Studios and all the storyboarding and recording was done there; but the more labor-intensive work was done overseas."

As Hanna proceeded to establish the overseas production facility, Joe Barbera remained in Los Angeles, overseeing storyboards and editing scripts. Barbera's duties also included directing recording sessions with the actors. Cast from a pool of radio talent that had been displaced with the advent of television, *The Flintstones* featured the voices of Alan

Reed as Fred, Mel Blanc as Barney, Bea Benadaret as Betty and Jean Vander Pyl as Wilma. (Five shows were actually produced with two other actors providing the voices of Fred and Barney, but were scrapped when Hanna and Barbera determined the characterizations were all wrong.) Recording sessions consisted of the cast convening at a table for one read-through of the script, and then proceeding to the microphones for recording. "We really had to be on our feet," Jean Vander Pyl recalled. "And that's why radio people were very valuable to the cartoon business – we had all been doing quick characterizations for twenty years."

When *The Flintstones* finally made its debut on ABC, audiences were charmed. Critics, however, were not. "*Variety* ran a headline that said, '*The Flintstones* is a pen-and-ink disaster,'" recalled Barbera. "But six years later, the disaster was still running in primetime. The public took it and made it a hit."

ABOVE: Fred and Wilma Flintstone's daughter Pebbles.

Indeed. Despite its eventual cancellation, the show continued to be a hit with the public – so much so that thirty-three years after its debut, Universal Studios and Amblin Entertainment committed themselves to a lavish, feature-length, live-action version of *The Flintstones*. It was an idea that appealed to Bill Hanna and Joe Barbera right from the beginning. "We were complimented and flattered that they would contemplate making a movie of *The Flintstones*," Hanna commented. "Both Joe and I were enthusiastic about it."

With Hanna-Barbera's full-fledged support, Amblin acquired the rights to the show in 1989. But while Amblin went on to other large-scale productions such as *Hook* and *Jurassic Park*, *The Flintstones* project remained in a kind of creative limbo. A key consideration in starting production on the movie

was John Goodman's schedule. From the project's inception no one but Goodman had been considered for the role of Fred Flintstone – in fact, the overall feeling at Amblin was that if John Goodman couldn't make the movie, it wouldn't be made. Goodman's commitment to *Roseanne* limited Amblin to a summer shooting schedule; and for several years, summers came and went without a start to production. The delay was due primarily to the fact that, despite numerous attempts by a variety of writers, a suitable *Flintstones* script had yet to be written. Finally, in November 1992, executive producer Kathleen Kennedy approached Spielberg on the set of *Jurassic Park* and suggested that if *The Flintstones* was going to be made the following summer, pre-production efforts would have to begin immediately. While a script was still not in hand, the decision was made to go forward with the project.

Production Team

Assigned to produce the film was Bruce Cohen. A first-time solo producer, Cohen had worked his way up through the ranks at Amblin, starting as a Director's Guild trainee on *The Color Purple*, serving

Director of a Comedy Series for his work on *The New Leave it to Beaver*. Following his feature film directing debut with *Problem Child II*, Levant had scored a huge hit with his second film, *Beethoven*, a Universal family comedy that grossed more than $143 million. Levant's most compelling qualification, however, was his lifelong obsession with *The Flintstones*. A collector of *Flintstones* memorabilia for seventeen years, Levant had been a fan of the show since his boyhood. "Growing up,"

as an assistant director on *Batteries Not Included*, *Always* and *Hook*, and finally going on to co-produce Frank Marshall's non-Amblin production, *Alive*. An associate producer who had just come off *Jurassic Park*, Colin Wilson was brought on to co-produce *The Flintstones* while Spielberg, Kennedy, Gerald R. Molen, Hanna, Barbera and David Kirschner all served as the film's executive producers.

DIRECTOR
Brian Levant

While yet another version of the script was being written, the production team turned to finding a director for the film, and eventually met with Brian Levant. A twenty-year veteran of television, Levant had written, directed and produced scores of episodes for Garry Marshall productions such as *Happy Days* and *Mork and Mindy*. In addition, Levant had received the 1989 ACE award for Best

Levant recalled, "I loved all the ABC television shows – *Leave it to Beaver*, *Donna Reed*, *Ozzie and Harriet*. And like everybody else in the country, I immediately recognized a true American original when *The Flintstones* came along. That show became an important part of my Friday nights; and I soaked it in, probably more than most people, just because of the relationship I had with the television medium." Ironically, Levant had actively pursued a shot

TOP: Steven Spielberg on set with John Goodman and Rick Moranis. ABOVE: Assigned to direct the film was Brian Levant a TV and movie writer-director who professed a lifelong obsession with *The Flintstones*. LEFT: Kathleen Kennedy and Bruce Cohen share a joke with Brian Levant.

at writing the *Flintstones* script from the time he had first heard the project was in the works.

"Every time word trickled down that they were looking for another script, I would call Amblin and tell them I was interested. But it was always, 'Sorry – we've already got someone working on it.' I tried again in the Fall of '92; and again I heard that the assignment had gone to someone else. But at that point the people at Amblin had seen *Beethoven* and were interested in me as a director. It seemed that my experience in family comedy and my lifelong interest in the *Flintstones* all added up, so they brought me on to direct, and eventually, they also let me write the script. I think they realized that, in me, they had someone who could restore the script to its roots and do a very faithful adaptation."

THE SCRIPT

Drawing on his television experience, Levant determined that the best way to write the *Flintstones* script was to gather a talented team of television comedy writers in the same room, and then let the gags fly. "We had a roomful of very creative people cracking jokes. Amblin provided us with a computer system that projected the script on a big screen, and we'd all talk it out and change things and throw things out – and watch it happen on the screen. Spielberg was editing *Jurassic* at the time and he'd come in for a couple of hours every day to drop in ideas. It was a really exciting, creative process."

What Levant and his writing team found missing in the previous

scripts was the innocence that had made the original *Flintstones* so appealing. "The *Flintstones* stories were really about friendship. There was a sense of forgiveness that permeated every episode and the characters all had great charm. But writers who are successful in a contemporary milieu tend to be embarrassed by material like that, so they write it off as silly and try to give it a kind of cynicism; and that is all wrong for the *Flintstones*, because the show is all about naivete. To me, *The Flintstones* was 1961; and the idea was to make it a 1961 sitcom. It is a style of television that I understand and love, so it was not a great departure for me."

Over a three-day weekend, the comedy writing team came up with a revised story for *The Flintstones*. Gaining Spielberg's enthusiastic approval on the following Monday, the writers spent fourteen days writing a first draft that incorporated Spielberg's suggestions, and then another twenty days polishing the final script. "We were able to get it done so quickly because that is what television writers know how to do – fix it and fix it now. In television, you turn out a new script every four days so we are accustomed to working fast."

Throughout the writing process, the Hanna-Barbera Studio had lent its support providing Amblin with story-boards from the original shows and fact-checking the script.

"We'd get these funny notes back from them that said, 'This person's name was actually so-and-so, and their street address was actually this,'" Bruce Cohen recalled. "At one point in he script we called Dino a dinosaur, and Hanna-Barbera said, "No, no – Dino is a dog." They also brought Wilma's mother, Pearl Slaghoople, to our attention – we'd given her the wrong name. And in one scene we'd mentioned beer; and they informed us that there was no beer in Bedrock, only Lava Juice. We loved those details because it helped us to make the movie as Flintstone-ized as possible."

ASSEMBLING THE TEAM

By the end of January, Amblin – after four years – at last had a script that captured the heart and soul of *The Flintstones*. Aiming for a shooting schedule that would begin in May, the production team turned its attention to the hiring of technical and creative personnel. For Brian Levant, a well-developed sense of the absurd was a prerequisite for working on the film. "Brian told me at the beginning that we had to hire crew members who were fun," Cohen noted. "And I said: 'What are you talking about? You can't hire crew people based on how good a sense of humor they have!' But, in fact, you can – and we did. I had never thought of it before, but Brian was absolutely right. We were making a comedy and we needed a funny set, with happy, funny people around. "We didn't discriminate against humor-impaired people, but we did try to keep a sense of humor in mind as we put the crew together."

Levant also looked for crew members who shared his passion for *The Flintstones*. "An enthusiasm for the project was everything to me," Levant said. "Our costume designer, Rosanna Norton, came to her interview wearing a snake skeleton necklace. Bill Sandell, our production designer, spends his free time riding in the desert, looking at rocks. We corralled all these interesting, *bent* people who, for one reason or another, felt they just had to do *The Flintstones*." Other key people brought onto the project – bent personalities one and all – were director of photography Dean Cundy, special effects coordinator Michael Lantieri, artist and puppeteers from the Henson Creature Shop and a digital team from Industrial Light & Magic, headed by visual effects supervisor Mark Dippe.

As the crew was being assembled, Levant and the production team began to cast the film, searching for actors who could do live-action justice to animated characters the world had known and loved for thirty years. While they had had their Fred Flintstone essentially since the day Spielberg had first approached John Goodman on the *Always* set, there remained the crucial casting of Barney, Wilma, Betty, Pebbles, Bamm-Bamm and Pearl Slaghoople – a modern Stone Age family.

THE STORY

Adhering to the themes of friendship so essential to the original, Levant and his writers devised a story in which Barney – in gratitude for Fred's help in adopting Bamm-Bamm – exchanges aptitude tests with his big-hearted, but somewhat dim-witted friend. As a result, Fred is promoted to vice president of the Slate & Co. quarry. The promotion is actually a plot hatched by junior executive Cliff Vandercave and sultry executive secretary Miss Stone who, after embezzling company funds through a dubious modernization scheme, plan to set Fred up to take the rap. Unaware that he is being used as a patsy, Fred enjoys wealth and an upwardly mobile status, while Barney is fired and drifts from one odd job to another. The friendship between the Flintstones and the Rubbles is severely strained until, finally, the embezzling scheme is uncovered. With the help of Wilma, the Rubbles and a sophisticated Dictabird who implicates the true villains, Fred's name is cleared and harmony is restored.

LEFT: As in the cartoon, the friendship between the Flintstones' and Rubble's (played by Rick Moranis, Rosie O'Donnell and Hlynur Marino Sigurdsson) was a vital element of the story.

"THEY'RE A MODERN STONE AGE FAMILY..."

CASTING

Casting for *The Flintstones* officially began after the production had received its green-light from Universal. In reality, however, the casting process had been going on for months, as Bruce Cohen, Brian Levant and the rest of the production team considered well-known actors as well as new names.

Of primary importance, obviously, was the casting of the Flintstones – Fred, Wilma and Pebbles – and their good friends and neighbors, Barney, Betty and Bamm-Bamm Rubble. As well-known and well-loved as the cartoon characters were, it was crucial that their live-action counterparts capture the essence of each character's personality and unique charm. Key supporting players were Cliff Vandercave, Miss Stone, Wilma's mother, Pearl Slaghoople, and Mr. Slate.

FRED FLINTSTONE
John Goodman

Throughout the *Flintstones* development phase, during which one *Flintstones* script after another was commissioned and rejected, there had remained one constant: no one but John Goodman was to play Fred Flintstone. "John Goodman was it," casting director Nancy Nayor commented. "In word association, if you said 'Fred Flintstone,' everyone would think, 'John Goodman.'"

Only Goodman himself had reservations. A versatile, well-respected actor, Goodman had turned in memorable performances in films such as *Sea of Love* (1989), *Raising Arizona* (1987), *The Big Easy* (1986) and *Barton Fink* (1991), for which he was nominated for a Golden Globe Award. Goodman was also no stranger to the theater, having been in the road company production of *The Robber Bridegroom* and on Broadway with *Loose Ends* and *Big River*. Since his move to television with *Roseanne*, Goodman had earned three Emmy nominations and three Golden Globe nominations for Best Actor in a Comedy Series. With such hard-earned recognition and stature, Goodman was initially reticent about identifying himself too closely with Fred.

"When Steven Spielberg first approached me about *The Flintstones*, I wasn't sure it was something I wanted to do, mainly because I was afraid of being type-cast as Fred Flintstone. As an actor, I didn't know if it was a smart move. I thought, 'If I do this, I'm going to have to kiss those Ibsen festivals goodbye."

John Goodman as Fred Flintstone. A renowned character actor, Goodman was handpicked by Steven Spielberg to bring the cartoon character to the big screen.

Brian Levant understood Goodman's hesitation in taking on the role. "John is a well-trained, really great actor, and I'm sure he was wondering if this career move meant he was going to be 'Yabba-Dabba-Dooing' for the rest of his life. But I think those fears were allayed when he read the final script and saw that Fred was a human being – albeit a human being whose every thought and feeling is externalized. There was a real character there, something he could sink his teeth into."

characters as one of the regular cast members of the highly-regarded SCTV television show, Moranis had gone on to star in films such as *Ghostbusters* (1984), *Little Shop of Horrors* (1986), *Honey, I Shrunk the Kids* (1989), and its sequel *Honey, I Blew Up the Kid* (1992). After years of following the *Flintstones* movie's progress with great interest, Moranis promptly came on board.

BARNEY RUBBLE
Rick Moranis

Securing a firm commitment from Goodman, the production team began considering actors for Barney. At the top of the list was Rick Moranis. A comedian and actor who had created a wide variety of

Comic actor Rick Moranis as Fred's bosom buddy Barney Rubble. The cameraderie and chemistry between Goodman and Moranis was crucial to the 'two buddies' structure of the movie.

Rosie O'Donnell as Betty Rubble and Elizabeth Perkins as Wilma Flintstone. A standup comedy favourite, O'Donnell had made her acting mark with supporting roles in *A League of Their Own* and *Sleepless in Seattle* before landing the part of Betty. A theatrically-trained actress, Perkins was best known for serious roles in films such as *Big*, *Avalon* and *The Doctor*.

what a big part they played. But when you actually go back and watch the shows, you find that they were surprisingly one-note. So we were a little disappointed when we turned to the cartoons for inspiration. We realized we were going to need more excitement in the women for the movie. "

WILMA
Elizabeth Perkins

Among those who auditioned for Wilma was Elizabeth Perkins, an actress who had distinguished herself in films such as *Big* (1988) and *Avalon* (1990), and had turned in a poignant dramatic performance as a terminal cancer patient in *The Doctor* (1991). "I'd always thought of her as a wonderful serious actress," Nayor commented, "but then she came into this audition and she was so funny and goofy – she just came to life in a way I'd never seen before."

In John Goodman and Rick Moranis, *The Flintstones* had its 'two buddies' so crucial to the story. With that central relationship determined, the filmmakers were able to begin casting Wilma and Betty – characters that were equally vital to the film, and yet rather vaguely defined in the original cartoon show. "When you remember Wilma and Betty from the animated show," Cohen noted, "you have a sense of what wonderful women they were, and

"Elizabeth was the only actress who came in with a worked-out character," Cohen agreed. "She actually read as Wilma which was a risk for her. But the minute she opened her mouth we all said, 'My God, there she is.' We really felt as if we had Wilma in the room."

Another thing going for Perkins was her enthusiasm for the project. "I was always interested," Perkins said. "It seemed to me that if you could do it right, it would be an amazing artistic and technical feat to bring an animated series to life; and I wanted to be a part of that. Also, it was a chance for me to do something that was completely different. There are very few roles for women as it is, and even fewer comedic roles. So something as broad and big and funny as *The Flintstones* was a real find."

BETTY
Rosie O'Donnell

Brian Levant's wife, Alison, was actually the first person to mention Rosie O'Donnell as a natural for Betty Rubble. It seemed, at first, an offbeat suggestion. A stand-up comedy favorite who had only recently made her acting debut in *A League of Their Own* (1992), O'Donnell's image was that of a tough, wise-cracking New Yorker with a heart of gold – hardly a description of Betty Rubble. Moreover, O'Donnell did not physically resemble the stick-thin animated image of Betty. "Rosie wasn't everybody's traditional idea of Betty," noted Cohen, "but Brian and I kind of liked that. And we were both tremendous fans of her comedy. So we decided to give her a shot; and when she came in to audition she was brilliant. She was Betty Rubble."

O'Donnell herself was amused at the creative casting. "When my agent called to tell me that I was one of the top considerations for Betty, I cracked up. I said, 'Are you kidding?' But then, every time I told someone that I might be Betty Rubble, there was this immediate reaction. Everyone laughed, and I began

to think maybe it wasn't such a weird idea. I thought, 'Okay, a chubby-ish Betty Rubble.'" In a sense, O'Donnell had been preparing for the audition all her life. "I'm a big TV trivia freak – I watched TV endlessly as a child – so I knew all the *Flintstones* episodes and I was very familiar with the Betty Rubble laugh. So at the reading, after every line, I would do Betty's laugh – because that was what I remembered most about her. In the cartoon, Betty wasn't as well defined as the other characters, so this was really the only thing I could grab on to."

Betty with the Mastodon – one of two-dozen creatures in the film provided by the Henson Creature Shop.

21

CLIFF VANDERCAVE
Kyle MacLachlan

With the four principals cast, the film makers began to concern themselves with supporting characters: odious executive Cliff Vandercave, sultry Miss Stone, Pebbles, Bamm-Bamm, and Wilma's mother, Pearl

The Flintstones' villains – who scheme to discredit Fred and embezzle funds from the Slate & Company Quarry – are secretary Miss Stone and executive Cliff Vandercave, played by Halle Berry and Kyle MacLachlan.

Slaghoople. Among those who read for Cliff Vandercave was Kyle MacLachlan, best known for his roles in David Lynch productions such as *Blue Velvet* (1986) and television's *Twin Peaks*. "I am a fan of the *Flintstones* cartoon," MacLachlan said, "so I went in and auditioned and had fun with it. Bruce and Brian, to their credit, made it a very easy and relaxed thing. I talked with them beforehand, asked them how broad I should go with this guy, and they said, 'We'll tell you if you go too far.' So I felt comfortable to just experiment during the audition. All those years watching cartoons probably helped."

"Kyle was the best out of everyone we read for that part," Cohen said, "which didn't surprise any of us. We had all loved his work in the past. He's handsome, but in an unconventional way. And he looks 'Flintstonian' – his chin is incredibly prehistoric."

MISS STONE
Halle Berry

While Kyle MacLachlan came in and won his role fairly early in the process, the casting of Miss Stone was a longer ordeal. The character's name in the script – Sharon Stone – had been a joking reference to the femme fatale star of *Basic Instinct*: but when it came time to cast, Cohen and Levant couldn't help but be tempted at the prospect of Sharon Stone playing the role herself. Stone was contacted and was delighted by the proposition, but because of commitments to other projects was forced to turn down the role.

With Sharon Stone no longer an option, the filmmakers went through a long auditioning process, eventually casting Halle Berry. A young actress who had starred in Eddie Murphy's *Boomerang* (1992) and had earned favorable notice in her television performance as *Queen*, Berry had come into the *Flintstones* audition with concerns as to the filmmakers' willingness to cast a black actress in the role.

"Before I auditioned," said Berry, "I sat down and talked with Brian Levant about the character; and I realized he was open to the idea of the character being black. But, in spite of that, and in spite of the fact that I felt good about my reading, I still left with the thought in my mind that they would never go black with this character. So when they called a couple of days later to say I got the part, I was really surprised."

Open casting calls which drew hundreds of four- and five-year-old twins resulted in the casting of Elaine and Melanie Silver as Pebbles, and Hlynur and Marino Sigurdsson as Bamm-Bamm.

PEBBLES AND BAMM-BAMM
The Silver and Sigurdsson Twins

The process of finding Pebbles, the Flintstones' red-haired daughter, and the Rubbles' untamed adopted son Bamm-Bamm involved open casting calls which drew literally hundreds of bone-adorned, loincloth-garbed four- and five-year-old twins. In addition to a physical resemblance to the cartoon Pebbles and Bamm-Bamm, Nayor was looking for an ability to understand directions and concentrate. "Even though they didn't have a lot of lines in the movie, it was important that they be able to focus. We were also looking for personality, and something in the eyes that would be interesting to watch."

For Bamm-Bamm, Nayor found Hlynur and Marino Sigurdsson. "They were Icelandic and they had this look that was sort of Neanderthal-like. They definitely didn't look like contemporary American children." Unlike the Sigurdsson twins, who had no previous acting experience, the twins pegged to play Pebbles – Elaine and Melanie Silver – had appeared in a recurring role on the daytime drama *General Hospital*. Naturally blond, the Silver twins' hair was tinted an appropriate Pebbles-red for the film.

PEARL SLAGHOOPLE
Elizabeth Taylor

The final supporting role to be cast was Pearl Slaghoople, Wilma's flamboyant mother – and the bane of Fred's existence. Although the deal was not finalized until shortly before filming began, the inspiration to cast Elizabeth Taylor in the role came very early. "Kathy Kennedy came to me one day in December," Cohen recalled, "and she said, 'I know who Pearl Slaghoople should be – Elizabeth Taylor.' And I said, 'You are a brilliant woman.' It was so perfect an idea. So she and I made a pact at that moment that no matter what happened, no matter what anyone told us, no matter what obstacles were thrown in our way, Elizabeth Taylor was going to be Pearl Slaghoople."

Ending a nearly fourteen-year absence from the big screen, Elizabeth Taylor brought her own inimitable style to the role of Pearl Slaghoople, Wilma's mother, seen below arguing with Fred while Wilma looks on.

A two-time Academy Award winner, Taylor had risen to nothing less than legendary status through a career which spanned several decades and included films such as *National Velvet* (1944), *Cleopatra* (1963), *Who's Afraid of Virginia Woolf?* (1966), *Cat on a Hot Tin Roof* (1958) and *Suddenly Last Summer* (1959). Committed to various humanitarian causes in recent years, Taylor had not acted in a film since appearing in 1980's *The Mirror Crack'd*. Fortunately for the *Flintstones* producers, however, Taylor had begun expressing an interest in returning to films just as the movie went into production.

"At the time," Cohen recalled, "she was looking for the right part; so we thought she might do it, but we never knew until the deal came together. We just kept up a running dialogue with her wonderful agent, Morgan Mason, through the whole casting process, and finally it happened."

B-52s

Another casting coup was realized with the signing of the alternate music group the B-52s – comprised of Kate Pierson, Fred Schneider and Keith Strickland – to perform both 'the Twitch' and their own version of the *Flintstones* theme song as the 'BC-52s'.

SUPPORTING PLAYERS

Rounding out the cast were *Night Court*'s Richard Moll as Hoagie, television favorite Irwin '88' Keyes as Joe Rockhead, character actor Dann Florek as Mr. Slate, former pro-football star Jack O'Halloran as the Neanderthal Yeti, Laraine Newman as a reporter for the Cave News Network, Sheryl Lee Ralph as Mrs. Pyrite, the adoption agency manager, and Jonathan Winters and Jay Leno in cameo appearances.

By the time production began in mid-May casting for *The Flintstones* was completed, but long before John Goodman shouted his first 'Yabba-Dabba-Doo' or Rosie O'Donnell emitted her first Betty Rubble giggle, production designer Bill Sandell and a veritable army of art directors, designers and illustrators were engaged in the daunting task of translating to three dimensions the entire world of the Flintstones .

TOP LEFT: Recording stars Fred Schneider, Kate Pierson and Keith Strickland – the B-52's – perform as the 'BC-52s' in a nightclub scene at the Cavern on the Green. TOP RIGHT: Jonathan Winters in a cameo role. BELOW: Appearing in supporting roles are Dann Florek as Mr Slate, Sheryl Lee Ralph as Mrs. Pyrite, Richard Moll and Irwin Keyes as quarry workers Hoagie and Joe Rockhead, and Laraine Newman as a reporter for CNN – the Cave News Network.

CHAPTER 3

"FROM THE TOWN OF BEDROCK ..."

PRODUCTION DESIGN

Because *The Flintstones* was to be an extra ordinarly large and complex assignment, the first order of business after the project had received its greenlight in November 1992 was the hiring of a production designer. There was no residential location that could double as the Flintstone and Rubble neighborhood. No town existed that looked anything like Bedrock; and no prop rental company had *Flintstone*-style dinnerware or stone newspapers or prehistoric strollers. Everything in *The Flintstones*, from Pebbles' baby spoons to the Stonehenge-inspired Cavern on the Green nightclub, was going to have to be designed and built from scratch. "Basically," Bruce Cohen commented, "there was no *Flintstones* movie without the production design. The set decorating, the costumes, the cars, even the cast, their makeup and hair, all had to come out of the production design."

PRODUCTION DESIGNER
William Sandell

Late in November, Levant and the producers hired William Sandell. A production designer with thirteen years' experience, Sandell had spearheaded the design efforts for films such as *Total Recall* (1990), *RoboCop* (1987) and *Hocus Pocus* (1993), and seemed ideally suited to take on *The Flintstones* assignment. Not only did Sandell have a penchant for visually startling and unusual films, he was also a longtime rock collector *and* a bonafide *Flintstones* fan. "I'd been looking for a movie like this all my life," Sandell said. "I hate doing reality movies. Who wants to see reality? I like doing films where you get to create something nobody has ever seen before. And *The Flintstones* was a chance to do that."

THE ART DEPARTMENT

Bringing aboard designers and craftsmen he had collaborated with on previous shows, Sandell established a design team that also included veterans of Amblin's art department. Because of the scope of the project, three art directors were assigned to the film: Nancy Patton, Chris Burian-Mohr and Jim Teegarden, a key art director at Amblin who had most recently contributed to *Jurassic Park* (1993). Another Amblin artist with a long list of credits to his name, Marty Kline joined *The Flintstones* project as production illustrator.

Rounding out this core group was a team of five set designers, set decorator Rosemary Brandenburg, costume designer Rosanna Norton and property master Russell Bobbitt.

"I had wonderful people supporting me," Sandell asserted. "Amblin is very aware of what an art department can do for a film. Their style is, 'If you've got a problem, work it out in the art department.' So they very graciously hired all of these talented people for me to interact with."

With the core group assembled, Sandell and his design team began to explore how to bring the flat, roughly-sketched world of the *Flintstones*

Among the largest exterior sets built for the production was the suburban neighborhood which was home to the Flintstone and Rubble families. LEFT: Suburban Bedrock under construction at Vasquez Rocks. BELOW LEFT: Production designer Bill Sandell with a model of the suburban neighborhood. BELOW: In addition to exteriors, a number of interior sets were built on soundstages at Universal Studios. Sandell and set decorator Rosemary Brandenburg confer on the interior set of the Slate & Co. headquarters lobby.

cartoon into three dimensions. "In the cartoon," Sandell commented, "they were allowed to get away with all kinds of discrepancies in volume and space. For example, Fred would run from Dino for what amounted to about a hundred yards inside his house. But we couldn't get away with that in three dimensions. So we had to come up with

29

designs that were cartoon-*like*, but still believable. We were walking a very fine line: too far one way, and we'd lose the reality of the story; too far the other way, and we'd ruin the joke."

Overall, the design team strove to recreate the *Flintstones'* visual style – which was, basically, to parody the designs of the early Sixties in rock and stone. To keep his department on the Stone Age track, Sandell took a page from the Clinton presidential campaign which had a sign at its headquarters reading, 'It's the Economy, Stupid.' Paraphrasing, Sandell's *Flintstones* art department banner read, 'It's Rock, Stupid.'

To get the design ball rolling, Marty Kline produced hundreds of pencil sketches – later rendered in color by Tim Flattery – depicting all things Flintstonian. Drawings of houses, furniture pieces, the Slate headquarters – virtually everything the film would require – were rendered and presented to Brian Levant for approvals.

The Flintstones' neighborhood. Included in the set were stone sidewalks and cartoon-like trees carved out of foam.

Bedrock

Of primary importance early in the design process were the variety of exterior sets called for in the script. Two Southern California locations were chosen as the sites for the main outdoor sets: downtown Bedrock, an outdoor bowling alley, a drive-in movie theater, and the Slate & Co. headquarters and quarry would be built at the CalMat rock quarry in Sun Valley – a huge working quarry which sat two hundred feet below the San Fernando Valley floor. Suburban Bedrock – where the Flintstones and Rubbles lived – would be erected at picturesque Vasquez Rocks in northern Los Angeles County.

Among the first sets to be designed was the Flintstones' and Rubbles' quiet suburban neighborhood which consisted of a single tree-lined street flanked by *Flintstone*-style houses with well-manicured lawns. "Even in the initial sketches," Marty Kline explained, "I tried to suggest the kind of *Flintstone* visual gags we might include in the set: I

ABOVE: The Flintstone home. All of the houses on the tree-lined street were designed to blend with the jutting rock backgrounds at Vasquez Rocks.
LEFT: Barney and Betty's house. Because they had to be built at Universal and then transported to the Vasquez location, all of the houses were constructed from light-weight foam.

early Sixties, California neighborhood would be. The design of the houses started with the idea that, in the *Flintstones*' time, houses would be built by taking a great big rock and hollowing it out, then cutting holes for doors and windows. We decided they would have rock chimneys and slab rock roofs. For the roofs, we tried to emulate the jutting rock look at Vasquez Rocks, so the homes would look as if they belonged in that environment.

put a basketball court in one of the driveways, and for the hoop I just drew a slab roof over the garage with a hole in it. The sketches also included stone skateboards, stone fire hydrants, stone street lamps, various kinds of cars, a stone catamaran in one of the driveways, kids dribbling a stone basketball – any visual gags I could think of."

Presented with Kline's sketched overview of suburban Bedrock, art director Jim Teegarden proceeded to pin down the specific look of the neighborhood. "We took each house," Teegarden explained, "and tried to give it a slightly individualized look, yet still make it tract-like, just as an

We chose organic earth tones for the color schemes – again, to make the houses fit in with the surroundings."

Going from sketches to colored renderings to, in some cases, small-scale models, and finally to blueprints, the house designs eventually wound up in the hands of construction supervisor Cal DiValerio. Because the authorities at Vasquez Rocks had afforded the production company use of the site for only a short period of time, all of the structures in suburban Bedrock had to be prefabricated at Universal Studios and then transported later.

"Because we knew we were going to have to transport everything," DiValerio explained, "we had to build these things as lightweight as possible. We also had to be able to take them apart and reassemble them." To that end, wooden armatures were bolted together, covered with aluminium screening to create a basic shape, and then covered with lightweight foam. "Our sculptors would come in and sculpt the foam into the appropriate irregular shapes. After that, we would paint them and cover them with a hard coat to protect the foam. We built seven of those houses at Universal; and then, twelve days before shooting started, we transported them to Vasquez Rocks."

Before the arrival of the structures at Vasquez, however, DiValerio's construction crew had spent weeks preparing the site. Pads of decomposed granite were prepared for each house, along with granite roads, pebble-like curbs and flagstone-style sidewalks. Lawns made of an appropriately bizarre variety of grass – grown by the greens crew months before the start of production – were also laid down in each yard. Added to the neighborhood foliage were fake trees that had been designed to reflect the cartoony *Flintstone* world.

Of primary concern throughout the preparation – and ultimately, the shoot – at Vasquez Rocks was the protection of the rare plant life found at the location. "We had to be very, very careful," Jim Teegarden asserted. "There were rangers out there supervising us ten hours a day, and they were very conscientious about their work. But there were no problems – we either stayed away from the plant life or we built around it."

When completed, the suburban Bedrock set at Vasquez Rocks was a quaint wonderland – a model tract neighborhood, *Flintstone*-style. "It was amazing," Sandell said. "Even those of us in the art department were stunned by it when we first saw it. You would drive over the hill, and there it was – beautiful and magical and looking as if it had been sitting there in those rocks for 20,000 years. The first time Steven Spielberg saw it, he was so moved by it that he came over and hugged me. He said, 'I have never, ever seen anything like this . . .'"

Like Vasquez Rocks, the CalMat quarry was an ideally rocky and Flintstonian-looking spot for filming. Surrounded by steep rock walls two hundred

ABOVE: The Slate & Co. headquarters was a massive edifice set against the steep rocky walls of the CalMat quarry in California's San Fernando Valley.
OPPOSITE: The rock quarry where Fred and Barney work.

feet high, the quarry also featured a number of rocky plateaux and, at its center, a beautiful clear lake. Among the sets constructed at the quarry was the Slate & Co. exterior, the setting for many of the film's key action sequences.

Construction of the building and surrounding quarry, as well as the giant rock slicer machine – the modernized equipment which, in the story, replaces the entire crew of Slate & Co. quarry workers – was well underway when an act of nature brought construction to a halt. After five dry years, California had finally ended its drought the previous winter with unusually heavy rainfall. The following spring – just as *The Flintstones* production began building at the quarry – water overflow was released from a nearby dam, causing underground water to rise from the quarry floor, sometimes at a rate of three to five feet per day. The production company soon

found its construction sites submerged in as much as thirty feet of water.

"The water rising in the quarry is funny now," commented art director Nancy Patton, "but it wasn't at the time. We had scouted the whole area and marked off where the quarry headquarters building and rock slicer would be. And two weeks later, the entire area we'd staked out was under water. So we marked out another location – and it happened again. At that point we were quite far along in the construction of the rock slicer; but we had to abandon everything, dismantle it and start all over again. The same thing happened with the headquarters building – we'd picked a spot that had this beautiful vista behind the building, and within a few weeks the entire thing was under water."

Building on higher ground, the production team eventually erected an imposing Slate headquarters

33

edifice made to look like black marbleized rock. Nearby, the rock quarry and rock slicer were constructed. Although authentic rocks were everywhere to be seen at the quarry location, lightweight foam replicas that could be easily lifted and moved were fashioned by the art department and used to dress the Slate & Co. quarry. To blend the cartoon-style rocks into the surroundings, both fake and authentic boulders were painted in muted colors and artfully positioned in the background. The quarry set also featured giant gates shaped like the skeletal ribs of a big prehistoric animal. To make the gates strong, heavy steel was welded together, then plastered and carved to look like bones.

The rock slicer machine, which figured prominently in the film's climax, had been conceived as a huge Rube Goldberg-like piece of Stone Age machinery. "Bill wanted a crank-and-gear-filled, whistly machine that would add suspense to the climax of the movie," Patton noted. "Marty Kline did sketches that broke down each piece of action, and then we got storyboards for the sequence. After we started getting an idea of what had to be in the rock slicer, I made an actual design model, keeping in mind that we couldn't use metal of any kind. It had stone wheels and reptile skins for conveyor belts, and shells for whistling vents. After I built that quarter-inch scale model, we

took it into the actual full-size design." Also constructed at the quarry was downtown Bedrock – a complete Flintstonian village that included Bank of Ameroka, Roc Donald's restaurant, Snob Auto (where the upscale Fred purchases a new Le Sabertooth 5000) the Brontley-Wontley Market, Toy-S-Aurus toy store, Marshy Fields department store, the adoption agency where Barney and Betty first meet Bamm-Bamm, a Chevrok gas station, and Jurassic Park, a quaint little play area with a dinosaur skull jungle gym and prehistoric animal swings. In addition, the quarry was home to a large outdoor bowling alley and the drive-in theater featured in the movie's opening sequence.

As with the residential area, the design of downtown Bedrock began with rough pencil sketches and brainstorming sessions between art department personnel and director Brian Levant. Art director Chris Burian-Mohr, in particular, concentrated on developing concepts for downtown Bedrock. One of the decisions made early on was to build the town as a finished, unified entity. Rather than build facades, the production design team created

four-walled buildings, laid out like a real town, with a main street and a central park. "We wanted to present it as an actual working community," Burian-Mohr commented, "to build the whole town and establish Bedrock as a unit. It gave everyone on the set a sense of cohesiveness, I think – as if Bedrock

was a real place where people lived and worked and shopped."

A relatively late addition to the town was the bowling alley. Because bowling scenes – and Fred's 'twinkle-toes' approach – had been beloved staples of the original cartoon, Brian Levant had been bothered by the fact that, as originally scripted, *The Flintstones* did not include a bowling scene. "We had a scene with Fred and Barney at their lodge, which was going to be a big phosphate cave, but there was no bowling in the script. It had seemed too costly a thing to do, to build another big interior set. But then, one day, I was looking at a *Flintstones* postcard and it was a picture of an outdoor bowling alley; and it was very simple – just rock walls and bleachers. So I ran to Bill Sandell and said, 'Look at this! There's the sky! They're bowling *outside*!' We had to cut a couple of other sets in order to find the money, but we were able to build the bowling alley, and we changed the lodge scene to a bowling scene."

LEFT: The CalMat quarry also served as the location for the downtown Bedrock. The exterior set including the Bank of Amerocka, Roc Donald's restaurant and several stores. ABOVE: Downtown Bedrock also featured Toy-S-Arus and a play area called Jurassic Park.

35

TOP and ABOVE: The Bowl-O-Rama set was a late addition to the production design agenda. In order to include bowling – and Fred's famous 'twinkle toes' approach – in the movie, a scene originally scripted to take place at Fred and Barney's lodge was re-written and set at the bowling alley.

With more than two hundred crew members working for three months – clear up to the first day of shooting – the town of Bedrock began to rise out of the gravelly floor of the quarry. Like the Slate headquarters, however, the set's location at the quarry had to be moved due to the continually rising water. "Luckily, the only thing we had done was lay everything out," DiValerio recalled. "We'd driven pegs in the ground to mark the area, and that's when water started coming up. So we moved Bedrock to a higher location on another plateau." Despite the water drainage problems, the construction of Bedrock was, logistically, an easier task than building at Vasquez Rocks had been. There was no plant life that had to be worked around, and the construction crew was able to build on site, rather than transport pre-fabricated buildings to the location. Because transportation of the buildings was not necessary, all of the Bedrock structures were built of durable plaster rather than lightweight foam.

Set Dressing

While painted backdrops sufficed to suggest the interiors of most of the downtown structures, the Toy-S-Aurus and Marshy Fields stores required extensive window dressing, provided by set decorator Rosemary Brandenburg. The window dressings, and all of the set dressings for the movie, would have to be created entirely from scratch.

"We couldn't just go and rent *anything*," Brandenburg commented. "Every single lamp, every piece of furniture, *everything* had to be thought about, designed, and then built."

Because the job was so far beyond the scope of a typical set decorating assignment, Brandenburg was given a small team of illustrators to conceptualize everything from lighting fixtures to Stone Age television sets.

"I had one illustrator who did nothing but watch the cartoons and sketch things. We found that the cartoons had great ideas, but design-wise they were not very well filled out."

Looking for inspiration, Brandenburg attended an annual rock show in Tuscon, collecting rocks of every size, shape and color. "Variety was important because we had so much stuff to make and it all had to be colorful and interesting. We looked at jade, granite, slate, red rocks, yellow rocks, green rocks, blue rocks, smooth rocks, rough rocks . . . And that helped us to begin thinking about colors and textures."

Adhering to the satirical style of the cartoon show, Brandenburg's set dressings reflected the styles of the Sixties more than authentic prehistoric themes. "I went through a lot of Fifties and Sixties books, looking for ideas. The shapes in the Fifties were so big and chunky, it was almost a natural progression to make them out of rock. I think a part of what made the original cartoon so funny was that the styles of the time were so easy to parody."

ABOVE: The opening and closing sequence – which recreated the cartoon's frame for frame – featured a drive-in theater set constructed at the CalMat quarry.
BELOW: Roc Donald's restaurant.

BELOW: Betty and Wilma window shop in front of the Marshy Fields department store. Everything from Stone Age toys to Flintstone-style jewelry and crystal had to be created for store interiors.

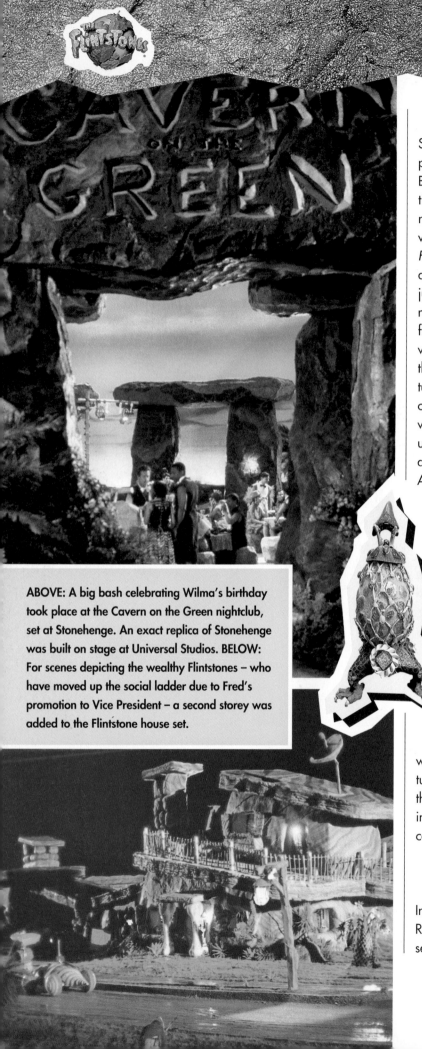

CAVERN ON THE GREEN

ABOVE: A big bash celebrating Wilma's birthday took place at the Cavern on the Green nightclub, set at Stonehenge. An exact replica of Stonehenge was built on stage at Universal Studios. BELOW: For scenes depicting the wealthy Flintstones – who have moved up the social ladder due to Fred's promotion to Vice President – a second storey was added to the Flintstone house set.

As designs were approved by Levant and Sandell, Brandenburg and her crew began building pieces that would furnish and decorate all the sets. Between Brandenburg's crew, DiValerio's construction crew and Russell Bobbitt's prop-making crew, nearly every available member of the various Hollywood crafts unions was commissioned to join *The Flintstones* production design effort. With as many as one hundred people on hand at any given time, just finding the space in which to work became a major logistical problem. "I had carpenters building frameworks, and sculptors buzzing away at things with their electric saws, and foam people spraying things with foam, and painters going wild with textures and colors – and we were all on top of each other. Foam particles would get into the paint, paint would spatter on everything. Finally, a big group of us cornered Paul Deason, our production manager, and screamed: 'More space! We need more space!' And we got more space."

For the storefront windows of Toy-S-Aurus and Marshy Fields, Brandenburg's team made *Flintstone*-style toys, rock crystal glassware, Faberge dinosaur eggs and jewelry. Also, because many of the downtown Bedrock scenes were to take place at night, the set decorators had to devise a wide variety of lighting fixtures for the Bedrock set. "We avoided simple torches for lighting fixtures. We wanted to suggest that they had gone beyond the torch stage and that they had some source of light – trapping zillions of fireflies and sticking them inside a lamp, or something like that. We left it vague, but we made it clear that it wasn't an open flame. We parodied every light fixture we could think of – pole lamps, chandeliers. In the bowling alley we had giant tusks that went up into the sky with a huge conglomeration of translucent rock hanging from it."

INTERIORS

In addition to the major exterior sets at Vasquez Rocks and the CalMat quarry, a number of interior sets were built on sound stages at Universal Studios.

Among the stage sets were the interiors of the Flintstone and Rubble houses, the Slate Company corporate offices, the interiors of the adoption agency and the department store, and Cavern on the Green – a posh nightclub/restaurant that was to be the setting of Wilma's birthday party.

It was during one of the many art department brainstorming sessions that someone suggested the idea of setting Cavern on the Green at Stonehenge. On Universal's large Stage 27, a full-size plaster replica of Stonehenge was constructed. To suggest an exterior landscape surrounding the club, a 240-foot-long, twenty-foot-high cyclorama was hung around the Cavern on the Green set. Jim Teegarden rendered an original sketch of the surrounding landscape that featured stylized volcanoes and a recreation of the aurora borealis. "It had a setting sun with a striation of red-orange," said Teegarden, "and then it went up into deep blues, with a kind of swirling pattern throughout the whole thing."

Teegarden was also instrumental in designing the interior sets for the Slate & Co. headquarters. Specifically, the script called for a boardroom, a lobby, offices for Fred, Cliff Vandercave and Miss Stone. The largest of the corporate building interiors, the boardroom, featured wall panels made to look like stone slabs. "We took wet sand," Teegarden explained, "and laid it on sheets of plastic that were the size and shape of panels. Then we foamed it, and the most amazing thing happened: when the hot foam hit the wet sand it created all these little fissures and valleys which looked wonderful. The next morning we pulled off the plastic, and then the painters came in and did a gentle overcoat of grey-black wash. As a final touch, they painted in gold veining."

The crew prepares the Slate & Co. lobby set for filming. The corporate headquarters featured parodies of paintings by artists such as Jackson Pollock and Andy Warhol.

For the interior set decoration of the Slate & Co. headquarters, a slick, Eighties, corporate raiders theme was chosen. "It was a lot of fun," said Brandenburg, "because we got to parody all the styles from the Eighties – the hard-edged, Italian glass stuff that came out during that time. Fred's office had a Rockintosh computer, complete with a real mouse that rolled around on a rock pad to manipulate things on the monitor. For his desk pad we made a big piece of 'dinosaur' hide with rocks at the corners. He had cute pencil holders and, of course, a 'Rockadex.'"

The corporate headquarters also featured modern art – parodies of works by abstract artists such as Jackson Pollock and Andy Warhol. Takeoffs of more traditional artists were also featured in the Flintstone and Rubble house interiors. "There isn't a cave painting anywhere in the movie," noted Brian Levant. "I didn't like the idea of a cave painting, or just a painting of a volcano – I wanted something funnier. So in the office building we have a Rockasso. And over the Flintstones' bed we hung a Stone Age version of Wyeth's 'Christina's World' – instead of the building off in the distance, there is a volcano. Also, in the living room we hung our version of Van Gogh's 'Sunflowers.'" As part of the gag, the art parodies were painted on what looked like slabs of stone to suggest that they had once been part of a cave wall and had subsequently been removed in one stone slab piece.

Interiors for the Flintstone and Rubble homes required some of the most extensive set dressings, including a 'working' rock television set with antler antennae, a giant prehistoric fish over the fireplace

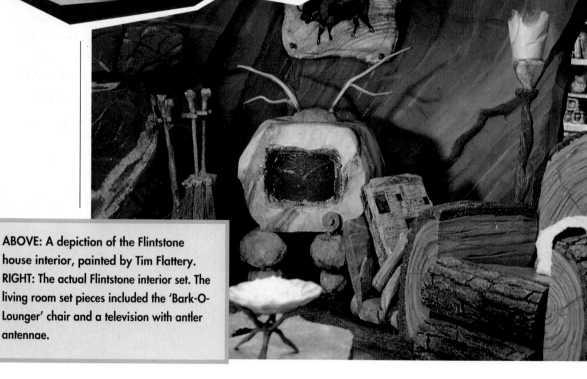

ABOVE: A depiction of the Flintstone house interior, painted by Tim Flattery.
RIGHT: The actual Flintstone interior set. The living room set pieces included the 'Bark-O-Lounger' chair and a television with antler antennae.

40

Although slightly smaller, the Rubble house also required ingenious dressing. To contrast with the Flintstone abode, the art department had designed an interior that reflected an undersea theme. "Shells and South Sea themes were very popular in the early Sixties," Brandenburg noted, "so it was appropriate. We had everything from sea kelp room dividers to seaweed rugs to a huge oyster for a bar top with shells at the base. The dining table had a giant sand dollar top and a star fish for the legs. Bamm-Bamm's crib was made out of four huge sea horses, and the sofa was a conglomerate of sea shells. Every sea creature we could think of, we made a joke of it."

mantel, and Sixties-style pole lamps with hide-covered shades. Furniture pieces were most commonly built by stripping existing pieces down to their frameworks, covering them with screen material and foam, and then sculpting the foam into the desired shape – a task headed by sculptor Yarek Alfer. A major consideration in the building of all the furniture was proportion.

"We made everything in the interiors bigger than lifesize, very rock-like and heavy," Sandell said. "At first, we were concerned that the furniture would diminish the actors in the scenes. In our first color tests and screen tests with the actors, I noticed that they were a little overpowered and I worried about it. But by the time we got to shooting, the costume department had bulked them up a little bit and they fit right in."

Of all the rooms inside the Flintstone house, the kitchen was among the most challenging, particularly since the set designers had opted for open cabinet shelving that revealed a variety of food products inside. Each food item – from Molten Oats Oatmeal to Good Eons Salad Dressing Mix – had to be a parody of an actual food brand. Thus, clever Flintstonian names had to be thought up, packaging logos had to be satirized, and each product had to be cleared through Universal's legal department.

ABOVE LEFT: Bamm-Bamm's bedroom reflected the ocean themes used throughout the Rubble house interiors. ABOVE: The Rubble's dining room featured a hanging jellyfish lamp. BELOW: An early sketch of the Flintstone house interior.

Props

Working in tandem with the art department and Rosemary Brandenburg was prop master Russell Bobbitt, who was charged with creating any item that was used by an actor or involved an action of some kind. "It is always a fine line between my job and the set decorator's job," Bobbitt commented. "For instance, a lamp sitting on a table in a scene would be Rosemary's responsibility; but if that lamp had to break, then it was mine."

Like Brandenburg, Bobbitt was faced with an unprecedented challenge in that every prop had to be manufactured. "Typically in a movie, the director says, I need a pen – and the prop guy runs to his truck and gets a pen. But in this case, every single item Brian needed took time, creativity, quick thinking, a drawing, an approval, a carpenter, a painter, a sculptor, a molder . . . I had two and a half months to prepare everything, which is more time than usual, but was still tight.

And, instead of the typical prop crew of three people, I had forty-four artists and crafts people working to produce props.

Among props manufactured for the movie were jewelry pieces that were worn by the actors. "We made a lot of rings that looked as if they were chiseled out of stone," Bobbitt said. "An illustrator came up with gorilla rings and rhino rings – all kinds of concepts – then, after getting approval from Brian, I took the drawings to a sculptor. He sculpted them out of clay; then we made

molds and cast them in resin. They then would go to the painters for detailing."

Watches were also worn by several of the main characters. "The watches were interesting because we had to figure out what a watch would be in the *Flintstones* world. So we made sundial watches – seventy or eighty different styles for all the different characters. We made the faces out of resin and then put stones and gems in as the numbers. For the actual sundial, I used triangular stones. The bands were made out of fake leather or bones or some kind of fake reptile, as if a little snake was actually holding the watch on the wrist." Elizabeth Taylor was so taken with the timepieces, she asked Bobbitt to make one specifically for her. "I made one up for her and we presented it to her at the end of the movie – along with a Cartier watch. It had purple stones on it and a leather band with some bones hanging off of it – smaller versions of the bones she wore in her hair. It flipped up, and there was a real watch underneath so she could actually use it."

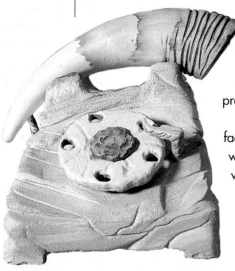

ABOVE: A Stone Age telephone. Every prop used in the movie had to be designed and built from scratch. ABOVE RIGHT: Spice rack from Wilma's kitchen. RIGHT: The prop crew also fashioned hundreds of pieces of Flintstone-style jewelry for the actors.

42

Another huge prop task was providing the dishes and glassware featured in the movie's dining scenes. Bobbitt fashioned resin martini glasses that looked like pink quartz, as well as ceramic dishes, silverware and coffee cups made to look like rough stoneware. Oversized food – both real and fake – was also required.

The first shot of the principal photography schedule, in fact, was a scene in which Wilma prepares a meal, cracking giant brontosaurus eggs into a cumbersome, oversized frying pan. A yellow resin yolk was placed inside a large, hard resin shell which was then injected with Methocel to simulate egg white. "We left a little piece of shell open," Bobbitt explained, "then glued that last piece on when the egg shell was filled. We had to score it so it would break when Wilma hit the edge of the pan. The egg also had to cook in the pan; and luckily, the Methocel turned white when it was heated, just like a real egg." Twenty-one brontosaurus eggs were made altogether, and all but one were used in the shooting of the scene.

ABOVE: Betty offers Barney deviled brontosaurus eggs. Both edible and fake oversized food items were created by the prop crew. LEFT: Wilma prepares a Fred Flintstone-sized breakfast. To simulate the giant brontosaurus eggs, yellow resin yolks and slimy clear Methocel were placed inside prescored resin egg shells.

For scenes in which the actors had to consume 'brontosaurus steaks,' Bobbitt procured whole sides of beef from a meat packing company, each of which yielded two to three giant steaks. The meat packing company also provided customized hot dogs that were sixteen inches long and an inch-and-a-half thick. "We also needed oversized vegetables for the salads. The first thing I did on the movie was call hot-house growers in Colorado to have them start growing huge tomatoes and heads of lettuce."

Also on the props agenda were stone-slab newspapers. "I made twenty newspapers, all of which had to have stories and headlines. One headline read, 'Pterodactyl crash in the Andes: Eats Rugby team to survive' – a spoof of *Alive*. There was also a story about Fred becoming a vice president. For that, we needed a picture of Fred. We went back and forth as to whether it should be a picture of John Goodman or a cartoon. Finally, it was decided to put in the actual cartoon face of Fred Flintstone, which was a fun twist."

Lettering for the newspapers – and all the worded items in the show – had been designed by the art department. Bobbitt had sets of letters in different sizes made up so that lettering could be stamped into foam props quickly and easily. "If the director wanted something on the spot – paperwork, a driver's license – I could just stamp these letters out and have the item immediately."

Altogether, Bobbitt and his crew produced nearly three thousand props: *Flintstone*-style musical instruments, Stone Age milk bottles,

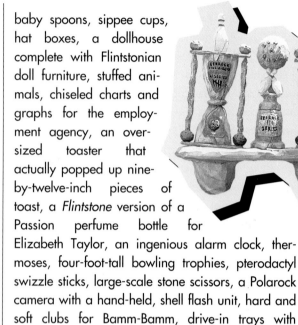

baby spoons, sippee cups, hat boxes, a dollhouse complete with Flintstonian doll furniture, stuffed animals, chiseled charts and graphs for the employment agency, an oversized toaster that actually popped up nine-by-twelve-inch pieces of toast, a *Flintstone* version of a Passion perfume bottle for Elizabeth Taylor, an ingenious alarm clock, thermoses, four-foot-tall bowling trophies, pterodactyl swizzle sticks, large-scale stone scissors, a Polarock camera with a hand-held, shell flash unit, hard and soft clubs for Bamm-Bamm, drive-in trays with Rocka-Cola cups, lightweight foam boulders, personalized license plates, a dental flosser used by Cliff Vandercave, signs for a quarry workers' strike, and hundreds of other items.

ABOVE: The movie required numerous magazines and stone slab copies of the 'Bedrock News'. TOP RIGHT: Bowling trophies. RIGHT: A Flintstonian record player featuring a rock turntable and a long-beaked bird built by the Henson Creature shop. INSET: A Flintstone version of a Passion perfume bottle.

44

Costume Design

An equally challenging design task was led by costume designer Rosanna Norton, an Academy Award nominee for her work on *Tron* (1982). "As soon as I got the movie," Bill Sandell said, "I called Rosanna. In my mind at least, she was the *only* person to design these costumes. I knew she'd bring something wonderful and unusual to the show."

Starting in January, Norton spent months researching *Flintstones* cartoons. "I kind of immersed myself into the *Flintstone* world," Norton said, "working on the problem of translating those drawn costumes and putting them on live human beings. I also thought about how to reflect the period of the early Sixties. I looked at all the Sixties fashion magazines; and also Sixties couture for scenes when the Flintstones become rich. I copied Dior and other designers of the era."

Norton began by drawing sketches, and then making costume samples for Brian Levant's approval. "It really helped to make the samples, because these things were so bizarre you really couldn't get a handle on them unless you could actually see them on a person. Colin Wilson and Bruce Cohen modeled all the men's dresses for us, and they looked great in them."

When it came time to actually build the costumes, Norton and her costume crew were limited to materials – or facsimiles of materials – that would have been available in the *Flintstones* world.

"We gave a lot of thought to what they would have used for thread, and eventually decided on some kind of gut. We also used little leather thongs, fur and leather. We actually used ultrasuede for the fur – we made a point of not using any real fur

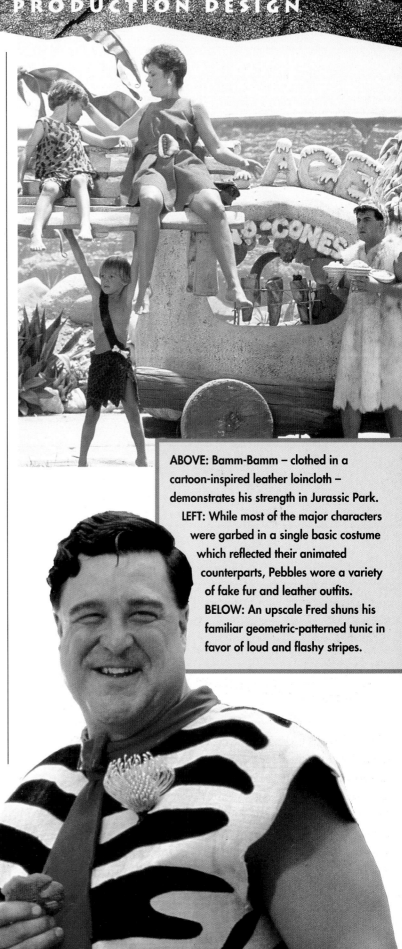

ABOVE: Bamm-Bamm – clothed in a cartoon-inspired leather loincloth – demonstrates his strength in Jurassic Park.
LEFT: While most of the major characters were garbed in a single basic costume which reflected their animated counterparts, Pebbles wore a variety of fake fur and leather outfits.
BELOW: An upscale Fred shuns his familiar geometric-patterned tunic in favor of loud and flashy stripes.

ABOVE: Fred and Wilma sport their everyday clothes. Throughout the film, all of the characters go barefoot. ABOVE RIGHT: Modified copies of Sixties couture fashions were created for Wilma's sophisticated look.

at all – and other materials that looked like snake skin."

Among the more difficult costume design tasks was Fred's familiar orange and black tunic. "It was hard to tell, from the cartoon, exactly what it was supposed to be. We couldn't tell if it was furry, or what kind of animal print it was. So we wound up making up a pattern that was a kind of Sixties-style, abstract leopard

print, and we printed that on ultra-suede." Although Fred wears the basic tunic throughout most of the movie, for scenes featuring the wealthy, upscale Fred, he sports a garish zebra-skin suit. "When Fred gets rich, he gets very loud – bright tiger prints and zebra skins."

Wilma, Betty and Barney were all outfitted in leather costumes that were virtual replicas of the garments the characters wore in the animated show. One wardrobe item Norton didn't have to contend with was shoes, since all the citizens of Bedrock go barefoot. "It was part of the joke – they'd be all dressed up with jewelry and hats and dresses, but no shoes. It could have been a really uncomfortable thing for the actors, walking barefoot out in that hot quarry, but everyone got into the spirit of it."

Once the designs were completed, Norton and a crew of twenty-five began building the costumes, working clear up to the end of the shoot. "Our last scene was at the Cavern on the Green nightclub, so we had to have all the costumes for the extras and the formal gowns and tuxedoes and everything. We wound up making close to two thousand costume pieces."

Through the talents of all the designers, crafts people and illustrators who made up the movie's production design team, the animated world of *The Flintstones* was successfully recreated for the live-action production.

"This movie was a major undertaking, and a major achievement from a design standpoint," co-producer Colin Wilson concluded. "And the production design team was so successful that when you see the movie you totally buy into this synthetic world. There are all these strange sets and cars and people in costume and all the sets are dressed with these wonderful props and set dressings; and as an audience member, you just buy into the whole thing and accept it. It is as if you are really in Bedrock yourself."

"There was a scene where I had to tie Elizabeth Taylor down with leather straps – as the prop guy, that was my job. So she came on to the set for the first time, and I was standing there with these leather straps and a shammy to put in her mouth for a gag. Nobody knew how she would react to being tied down; but it was my job, so I just calmly stood there and said, 'I'm going to tie you down.' And she looked at me and said, 'Men have been trying to do this to me for thirty years!'"

Russell Bobbitt, prop master

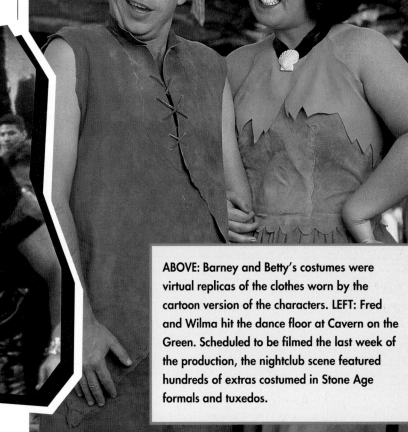

ABOVE: Barney and Betty's costumes were virtual replicas of the clothes worn by the cartoon version of the characters. LEFT: Fred and Wilma hit the dance floor at Cavern on the Green. Scheduled to be filmed the last week of the production, the nightclub scene featured hundreds of extras costumed in Stone Age formals and tuxedos.

47

CHAPTER 4

"THEY'RE A PAGE RIGHT OUT OF HISTORY..."

CREATURES

O f all the visual and verbal gags featured in the original *Flintstones* cartoon, the most fondly remembered are the whimsical prehistoric animals that performed duties as modern day appliances. From Fred's gentle Bronto-crane, to the mastodon that resignedly served as the Flintstones' kitchen faucet, the *Flintstone* creatures were crucial to the live-action film. Altogether, more than twenty creatures were called for in the script, including the Dictabird which was a prominent character in the story, and of course Dino, the Flintstones' rambunctious, dog-like pet dinosaur. Creating the vast majority of the creatures was a job that fell to Jim Henson's Creature Shop.

The Henson Creature Shop

"We knew from the beginning that we wanted the creatures actually on the set to interact with the actors," Bruce Cohen commented. "So we thought 'puppets' which, of course, immediately made us think 'Henson.'"

Established in London more than thirteen years ago, the Henson Creature Shop had provided characters for a wide range of films such as *Teenage Mutant Ninja Turtles*, *The Dark Crystal* and *Labyrinth*, as well as the *Dinosaurs* television show. Pioneers in puppeteering techniques who had won a technical achievement Academy Award for their computer-based Henson Performance Control System, the artisans at the Creature Shop were renowned for their ability to create fully-realized puppet characterizations and performances that were believable, funny and endearing – exactly

Jim Henson's Creature Shop was assigned the task of providing 24 Flintstonian creatures, including the mastodon faucet (BELOW) and the pigasaurus (RIGHT). All the creatures were sculpted in clay, then reproduced with silicone or latex skins covering mechanical understructures.

the qualities the *Flintstones* creatures would require.

Coming onto the project in February, the Henson Creature Shop had an extraordinarily large number of creatures to deliver by the time filming began in mid-May.

"We gave them only twelve to fourteen weeks to design and build twenty-four different creatures," noted Colin Wilson, who was primarily responsible for overseeing the creature effects effort. "Hanna-Barbera had given us a 'gadget and creature book' which had everything that had ever been in the cartoon, and we started with that reference material to help us keep to the original *Flintstones* style. We didn't want to go too far off into uncharted territory – although we did adapt the creatures to fit into a three-dimensional world."

To begin the design of the creatures, designer Jamie Courtier and Creature Shop supervisor John Stephenson flew to Los Angeles early in February to confer with Wilson, Cohen and Levant. "Basically," said Stephenson, "we were locked in an office at Amblin for a week with Jamie turning out drawings endlessly until we had determined a basic style."

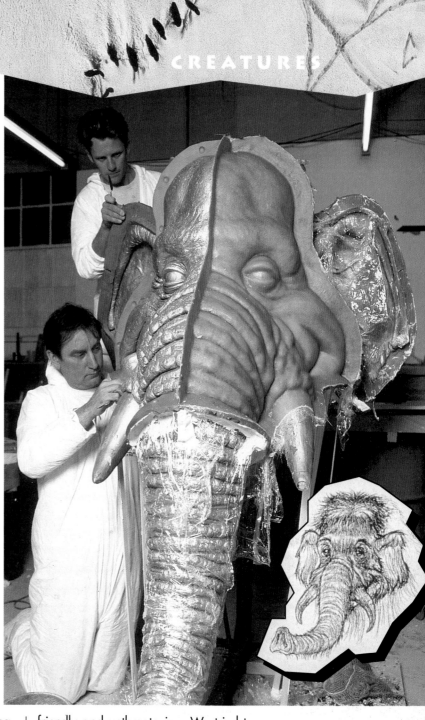

Returning to London, Courtier continued to fax drawings to Amblin for another few weeks, refining the look of the creatures as he integrated Levant's input. All the creatures had to have a certain warmth to them in terms of their expressions," Courtier said. "They had to look friendly and unthreatening. We tried to pay a certain allegiance to the original designs, while pushing them more into the realm of reality."

After securing final approvals on the drawn designs, the Creature Shop sculpted maquettes for all the major characters – six-inch clay models which were fully painted and

ABOVE: Creature Shop crew members at work on the full-scale Mastodon.
LEFT: During the creature design process, Creature Shop artists faxed dozens of renderings to Amblin for the production team's approval, finally building the approved designs as small six-inch maquettes. Shown are two maquettes and a rough drawing for the pigasaurus.

51

detailed. With Levant's approvals of the figures, the Creature Shop began replicating them in full scale. Construction of the creatures consisted of producing full-scale clay sculptures from which molds were made for the laying up of silicone or latex skins. The skins were then put over mechanical understructures engineered by the Creature Shop's mechanical department.

By far the largest creature built for the film was the full-size Bronto-crane featured at the Slate & Co. quarry and at the drive-in theater in the movie's opening sequence. Because wide shots of the full-bodied brontos were slated to be produced as computer generated elements, only those sections of the sixty-five-foot-long Henson bronto rig that would appear in more tightly-framed shots were fully skinned and painted. The finished head-and-neck section of the rig was employed for shots of the Bronto-crane picking up boulders at the quarry while the hump-like back was needed for shots of Fred atop the animal, working big-rig type controls. Two versions of the tail were built – one mechanized to sway back and forth, and another rigid fiberglass version used in the shot – made famous in the television series – of Fred sliding down the animal's tail and into his waiting car as his work day grinds to an end.

As devised by mechanical bronto supervisor Verner Gresty, the Bronto-crane had

ABOVE and BELOW: The largest of the Henson creatures was the Bronto-crane. The sixty-five foot long rig was equipped with two tails – a rigid fiberglass version and a mechanical version that could swish back and forth. RIGHT: The Bronto-crane's animatronic head under construction.

an animatronic head which sat atop a long cable-operated neck. "The neck was rigged with winches and pulleys," noted mechanical supervisor Chris Barton, "and it took a team of eight puppeteers to operate it."

For shots of Fred atop the animal's back, a simpler rocking mechanism that would suggest a general movement of the animal was engaged, while a forward movement was provided by mounting the entire Bronto-crane rig onto a track laid down on location by Michael Lantieri's special effects team. "Michael's team also arranged for a large crane to be on hand on location, so we could pick the whole rig up and move it from one place in the quarry to another."

Playing a major speaking role in the film was the Dictabird which acts as a kind of comic foil for Fred, but ultimately saves the day. A parrot-like, prehistoric dictating machine that measured a little over one foot long, with a wingspan of approximately thirty-six inches, the Dictabird was featured in a variety of scenes and situations throughout the film. "Adaptability was key to the Dictabird's design,"

ABOVE LEFT: A Creature Shop crew member finalizes the paint job on the Bronto-crane head. **ABOVE:** The Bronto-crane in action at Vasquez Rocks. A team of eight to eleven puppeteers was required to maneuver the giant rig. **BELOW:** The animatronic head was equipped with an articulated jaw to facilitate shots of the Bronto-crane lifting and carrying giant boulders at the quarry.

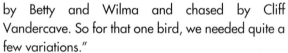

ABOVE: On location, the crew films the Dictabird in flight. Several versions – animatronic, radio-controlled and cable-operated – were built to afford the filmmakers as much flexibility on the set as possible. BELOW: Production crew members and puppeteers prepare for a Dictabird scene. Up to five puppeteers were required to operate the creature's various functions.

Barton noted. "It stands on a perch near Fred's desk throughout most of the movie, but it is also carried around by Betty and Wilma and chased by Cliff Vandercave. So for that one bird, we needed quite a few variations."

The Creature Shop constructed a modular puppet that could be fitted with interchangeable heads, necks and bodies. "We built two identical animatronic heads that had quite a bit of movement, one for backup in case there was a breakdown. As it turned out, we hardly used the backup head because this thing was impeccable in its performance. We also had a simple stunt head for long shots. We built two cabled bodies and a radio control body that could accept either the animatronic head or the stunt head. The radio control body was used for scenes where the bird was being carried around so that you wouldn't see any cables coming out of it."

Another version of the Dictabird was mounted on a pole arm and had cable-controlled running legs. "One puppeteer would support the body itself on a pole arm, and another puppeteer would operate a complete set of flapping wings, while another

controlled the running legs. So, for any given situation, a combination of these things could be put together to get the most out of the puppet for that particular shot. At its most complex it required up to five people to operate."

Operated by lead puppeteer Anthony Asbury, the Dictabird's animatronic head was controlled by the Henson Performance Control System – a computerized system which enables a single puppeteer to control a number of mechanisms to create complex movements and expressions. "The system has a joystick with output controls that go into the computer, and then into the creature," Barton explained. "The puppeteer can set up expressions – happy, sad, angry, whatever – and program them into the computer. And by moving the joystick to certain positions, he can create those expressions on the creature automatically. Those preset expressions can also be overridden by the puppeteer, so he

has a lot of freedom and creativity as he is going through a performance."

In addition to the Bronto-crane and the Dictabird, the Henson team was originally to be responsible for the creation of Dino. From the outset, the character had been difficult to conceptualize and execute. "Dino is really off the beaten track," Courtier commented. "No one is quite sure *what* he is. He's not exactly a dinosaur, not exactly a dog, not exactly human – but kind of a weird combination of all three. Plus, in the cartoon, Dino changed like a genie according to what they wanted him to do in the story. If he was giving the kids a ride on his back, he was enormous; but then, in another scene, Fred would hold him in his lap and he would

ABOVE LEFT: A kind of comic foil for Fred throughout most of the movie, the wise-cracking Dictabird ultimately saves the day. BELOW: The Creature Shop also built a fully animatronic Dino head for the closeups of the Flintstone family pet.

be like a small puppy. From a design standpoint, it was very difficult to pin Dino down."

No one had ever created an independent, completely animatronic puppet that would run into a room, wag its tail, and knock its master down with frenetic licking and pawing. Because of the complexity of the actions Dino would have to perform, it had been determined early on that the only way to realize the character was with a performer inside a 'Dino' suit. Design-wise, the man-in-a-suit approach was extremely limiting, since the concept of the character would have to conform to the basic anatomy of the human body.

After much back-and-forth conferencing with the production staff at Amblin, a foam rubber suit was constructed for Dino performer Dave Foreman. Foreman's legs would fit into the back legs of the suit, his arms holding on to leg extensions which came up from inside the suit's front legs. The entire suit was then topped with an animatronic head.

Despite Foreman's well-executed performance inside the suit, two weeks into shooting it was clear that the man-in-a-suit approach was inadequate to realize the important character of Dino. "We couldn't get away from the fact that no matter what you did with a human inside a Dino suit, it still looked like a man in a suit," Bruce Cohen commen-

TOP: Dino begging. Full body shots were achieved as computer graphic (CG) elements created by Industrial Light & Magic. RIGHT: Prop Master Russell Bobbitt arranges Dino's steak, while puppeteer Anthony Asbury prepares for a shot.

ted. "There was just no magic to it – and Dino, especially, had to have magic."

Conferences with the computer graphics department at Industrial Light & Magic led to the decision to render full-body Dino shots through computer graphics, while still employing a Henson Dino head puppet for closeups. Now freed from the constraints of human anatomy, Jamie Courtier literally went back to the drawing board and redesigned the character.

"We produced a new maquette that was more faithful to the original cartoon," Courtier explained. "Once we no longer had to worry about putting a man inside, we could design something that was closer to the original."

Working on *The Flintstones* up to the last day of shooting in August, the Henson Creature Shop team realized an array of Flintstonian creatures, including a stegosaurus time clock, a whistle bird, a reptilian creature which powers the Slate & Co. elevator, the Pigasaurus garbage disposal, a rodent razor, a mastodon shower and faucet, and a lobster lawnmower. "It was the shortest schedule we've ever worked under," Chris Barton commented, "but it was an altogether wonderful experience. The whole production crew was terrific; and for all the ups and downs, we had a great time."

Brian Levant was particularly pleased with the Henson team's contribution to his film. "The Henson people are wonderful – they are real artists who know how to create a performance. They were so creative and talented; and yet they understood that the creatures couldn't overpower the movie. I never wanted the movie to be about garbage disposals or Bronto-cranes. All of that stuff was accent – and the Henson group did it beautifully."

ABOVE: A sculptor adds texture to the 'skin' of the mastodon. **BELOW:** The Creature Shop provided a number of 'background' characters, such as the spiny prehistoric fish used in the Bedrock Adoption Agency scene.

BELOW: A modeler creating a resin mold for the spiny fish. **LEFT:** Another Henson Creature Shop creation – a working lobster lawn mower.

Industrial Light & Magic Computer Graphics

What could not be achieved on the set with the Henson puppets was realized by the computer graphics team at Industrial Light & Magic. Established by George Lucas in 1975, ILM had been a leader in the visual effects field for almost twenty years, and had, in recent years, distinguished itself with the creation of groundbreaking digital effects for *The Abyss*, *Terminator 2* and *Jurassic Park*.

At the outset of the *Flintstones* project, ILM had been assigned nine computer generated shots: a shot of Loch Ness-type monsters frolicking in a lake for an opening airborne approach of Bedrock; shots of a pterodactyl airliner; long shots of Bronto-cranes working in the quarry; and a smattering of digital wire removal shots to disguise puppeteering and special effects rigs.

Shortly into the production schedule, however, the computer graphics (CG) assignment grew to include sixteen full-body shots of Dino, as well as seven shots of Kitty – the Flintstones' sabertooth tiger pet – for a grand total of approximately forty shots. "The show tripled in size," said visual effects producer Judith Weaver, "and so we had to take on additional staff. We wound up with a crew of between twenty and thirty people working on *The Flintstones*. This was my first time out as visual effects producer and it was supposed to be my little training bra show with only nine shots – by the time it was over, it turned into a size DD."

Supervising the (CG) effort was Mark Dippe, an ILM veteran who had served as visual effects co-supervisor on *Jurassic Park*, a landmark film in which photorealistic, three-dimensional computer generated dinosaurs had been stunningly realized. While the remarkable technical achievements of *Jurassic* would serve ILM well, creating computer generated characters for *The Flintstones* required an entirely different mind-set.

"Character performance animation is very different from reality animation," Colin Wilson commented. "And in some ways, I think it was more difficult. ILM didn't have to go through the same learning curve they had in *Jurassic Park*, but just getting these characters to perform was really tricky. Bringing cartoon characters to life and into three dimensions created a whole new set of parameters."

Employing techniques and software they had developed for *Jurassic*, ILM began creating their CG characters as soon as the *Flintstones* production was in full swing. The first step was modeling, a process in which a three-dimensional model is built in the computer. While still in wire-frame form, that model is animated, then rendered as a finished, skin-covered figure; finally, more detailed bumps and surface textures are painted on through computer paint

ABOVE: ILM shots of Bronto-cranes at work. BELOW: For the opening sequence when Fred jumps into his car, John Goodman was filmed in reverse being lifted from the car by a crane.

ABOVE: Practical shots of the Bronto-crane were achieved by the full-size rig.
BELOW: The same view complete with ILM's computer-generated imagery.

character was Dino. After taking photographs of the revised Henson maquette from a number of different angles, the photographs were scanned into the computer as a starting point for the modeling process. "We traced the outlines of the photographs in order to digitize the shape," explained CG supervisor Alex Seiden. "It sounds very technical, but there is actually a lot of artistry involved. You have to be a very good sculptor to build something like that into the computer."

To determine the Dino model's actions, Dippe and the CG team studied both cartoon and live-action reference footage. "We wound up exaggerating Dino's movements so that they were more cartoon-like than anything a real dog could do," noted Dippe. "There was one shot, for example, where he jumped up and started to run, leaping into the air with his legs spinning underneath him. One of the advantages of CG was that we were able to

TOP and ABOVE: In a recreation of the cartoon show, *The Flintstones* included scenes of Dino frenetically greeting Fred. On set, John Goodman pantomimed his reaction to the pet, and ILM then matched the timing of his actions when inserting the computer generated imagery.

programs and customized texture maps. The final step is to composite the CG character with background plates shot on the live-action sets.

The most prominently featured CG

make him do things that were not realistic, but really fit in with the style of the movie."

Another key Dino shot was a recreation of the familiar scene in which Dino excitedly greets Fred at the door, chasing him and finally knocking him down and licking his face. For the shot, John Goodman had simulated being knocked backwards, and had then pantomimed his physical reactions to the overzealous pet. The computer generated Dino was then put into the scene. "I was amazed by Goodman's acting ability," Dippe commented. "We'd talk to him about what we needed from him to really sell the shot, and he would just do it. He really made it look like Dino was there on top of him."

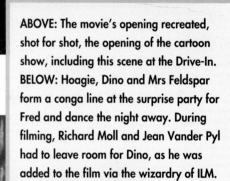

ABOVE: The movie's opening recreated, shot for shot, the opening of the cartoon show, including this scene at the Drive-In. BELOW: Hoagie, Dino and Mrs Feldspar form a conga line at the surprise party for Fred and dance the night away. During filming, Richard Moll and Jean Vander Pyl had to leave room for Dino, as he was added to the film via the wizardry of ILM.

Although far less prominent in the film, the character of Kitty proved to be one of ILM's biggest challenges on the show. As they had for Dino, the Henson Creature Shop had built a Kitty suit to perform on the set. Ultimately, however, it was decided that computer graphics could provide a more realistic character. The difficulty for ILM was that no one had ever successfully produced a fur-covered computer generated creature before. All of their research and development had, up until this time, been devoted to creatures with relatively smooth hides or skins. Creating CG fur was another matter altogether.

"The problem in creating fur," Dippe explained, "was that it has a very different kind of dynamic than skin has – it moves and changes direction as the animal moves, and its characteristics change according to where it is on the animal, or how light hits it, or whether or not it is wet or dry. It is really a complex thing to replicate."

"It was a hugely ambitious project for us," Judith Weaver elaborated, "especially given the time-frame. Mark and I committed to it on the set, then came back to ILM and said: 'Guess what, everybody? We're going to do fur!' and the whole software group gasped. But we were in it by then; we'd even shot the background plates already. We shot pretty wide plates so we wouldn't have to get in too close – we'd at least covered ourselves that way – but in the end, Brian didn't like the wide shot and we wound up having to move in much closer on Kitty than we'd originally planned."

After months of labor-intensive work involving the development of new software and new applications of digital techniques, ILM succeeded in producing the first completely computer generated, three-dimensional fur character.

Another groundbreaking digital contribution to *The Flintstones* is evident in the opening sequence. In what was dubbed the 'Powers of 10' shot, the camera moves into the movie screen at a drive-in theater featured in the re-creation of the cartoon's famous opening sequence. As the camera advances, it appears to move through clouds and over a rocky terrain which features a lake inhabited by two 'Nessies' – reptilian, Loch Ness-type monsters – and then up to a sign announcing 'Bedrock: First with Fire,' with the bustling prehistoric town of Bedrock in the distant background.

The Powers of 10 shot was made up of several elements: real clouds shot from a Lear jet, computer generated clouds, a helicopter flyby shot photographed at Lake Powell, computer generated Nessies, and a miniature of Bedrock complete with CG cars. "It is one continuous shot," Dippe noted, "that goes on for forty-five seconds – the longest digital shot we've ever done. I would say that it is prob-

RIGHT: As part of the opening sequence, the camera moves into the drive-in theater screen and through clouds to produce the view of a Triassic World Airlines pterodactyl airliner approaching Bedrock.

ably the longest digital shot anybody has ever done that combined live-action with three-dimensional, computer generated characters."

Also included in the opening sequence was a shot of the airborne pterodactyl airliner with more than a dozen Stone Age passengers aboard. While the cabin and passengers had been shot on a blue-screen stage – with the cabin mounted to a gimbaled rig to provide a rocking and rolling motion – the pterodactyl was a computer generated character that was combined with the bluescreen footage. Also computer generated were the colorful Nessies, designed by ILM art director TyRuben Ellingson, that were integrated with the Lake Powell footage. "In the shot," said Dippe, "you fly right by their heads, so you get a really dramatic view of these animals.

ABOVE: The 'Univershell' logo featured on the drive-in movie theater screen. BELOW: The opening sequence comes to a stop with this scene, complete with the bustling city of Bedrock in the background created by ILM.

They are very colorful and spectacular, with strong patterning."

Wide views of the Bronto-cranes working in the quarry were also produced at ILM. "The Bronto-crane shots were among my favorites in the movie," Dippe said. "They are wonderful wide shots that show these gigantic beasts moving slowly through the quarry, picking up rocks and dropping them. It is another example of what computer graphics can do: you can make these huge creatures that are so heavy and so photographically real – and you couldn't achieve that with a practical rig."

In addition to their creature work, the CG team was responsible for the digital removal of wires, rods, special effects rigs and, in some extreme cases, even puppeteers. Basically, digital rod removal involves a painstaking process in which scanned-in imagery surrounding the offending rig or wire is

63

replicated and patched in to create a continuous background. To make the filled-in area blend believably with the real background, shadows or lighting highlights must often be painted on by hand through a computer paint system.

"Some of the removals were quite painful," Dippe noted, "and they took a lot of creative thinking and diligence. There was one plate, for instance, where the puppeteers controlling the Dictabird filled far more of the frame than the bird did. By the time we were done with it, there was only the bird in the frame – and it looked flawless." In total, ILM executed thirty rod and wire removals for *The Flintstones*.

Through ILM's efforts, *The Flintstones* was populated with characters that could not have been realized as believably any other way. Brian Levant, a director who was, by his own admission, a novice in the computer graphics field, came to appreciate the tremendous creative freedom CG can offer. "In the beginning, I was really in the dark about this stuff. In fact, we'd already committed

much of the movie to CG, and I'd still never even *seen* a completely computer generated character – this was before *Jurassic* came out. But I watched, I listened, and eventually I caught on. And as completed shots started to come down from ILM, I became more and more excited."

Helicopter footage of Lake Powell was combined with computer generated imagery from Industrial Light & Magic to create this wonderful scene of 'Nessies' frolicking in the lake.

CHAPTER 5

"LET'S RIDE WITH THAT FAMILY DOWN THE STREET, THROUGH THE COURTESY OF FRED'S TWO FEET..."

SPECIAL EFFECTS

I t is a comical, familiar sight in the *Flintstones* cartoon: Fred jumps into his wood-frame, boulder-wheeled car and, pedaling his feet as fast as he can, takes off at a literally running speed.

SPECIAL EFFECTS COORDINATOR
Michael Lantieri

Translating that cartoon image to live-action was just one of the tasks that fell to special effects co-ordinator Michael Lantieri. While the art department had designed the *Flintstone*-style bowling alley and modernized rock slicer machine, it was Lantieri's job to make the ball and pin returns work, and to make the rock slicer slice. Prop and set dressing departments had constructed clever-looking cigarette lighters, but it was Lantieri's ingenuity that made the lighter light. The artisans at Henson and ILM had provided wonderful three-dimensional puppet and computer graphic characters, but the mastodon faucet would not have spewed water, and the computer generated Dino's physical presence on the set would not have been believable without Lantieri's contribution.

A longtime collaborator on Amblin productions with multiple Academy Award nominations, Lantieri had provided the special effects for films such as *Who Framed Roger Rabbit*, *Hook* and *Jurassic Park*.

Stone Age Cars

Coming onto *The Flintstones* early into preproduction, Lantieri first turned his attention to the variety of *Flintstone*-style cars that would be featured in the film, among them Fred's familiar 'steam-roller' model, Barney's pencil-like vehicle, Cliff Vandercave's flashy Mersandes, the Le Sabertooth 5000 sportscar purchased by the high-rolling Fred, Pearl's conch-shaped car, and background vehicles such as buses and an ice cream truck.

Altogether, the special effects team would build twenty-some vehicles. Steel mesh under-structures were sprayed with foam, then carved and painted to achieve the desired look. While the less prominently featured vehicles were either pushed or pulled by cables, the hero models were equipped with battery-driven, upgraded golf-cart motors, and motorboat steering mechanisms. "The cars could get up to about twenty-five miles an hour," Lantieri noted, "which was pretty fast for something made out of foam."

Undoubtedly the most recognizable of all the vehicles was Fred's foot-powered sedan. "To build Fred's car," Lantieri said, "we started with a toy *Flintstone* car that Brian gave us, which was the classic rag-top model. It was the hardest one to build because it had big granite steamroller wheels in

BELOW: Key production personel from L-R: Michael Lantieri, SPFX coordinator, Chris Burien-Mohr, Art Director, Paul Deason, Production Manager, Angela Heald, Production Coordinator, Jim Teegarden, Art Director, Colin Wilson, Co-Producer, and Marty Klein, Art Director. RIGHT: The sno-cone truck, Flintstone-style.

ABOVE: Brian Levant confers with John Goodman and Rick Moranis prior to shooting an opening scene in which Fred and Barney return home from work.
LEFT: The famous Flintmobile.
BELOW: Barney's pencil-shaped vehicle was modified as a two-log design to accommodate more passengers.

the front and back. The biggest problem was just coming up with a way to turn it, which we eventually achieved with cables and gears." To simulate the big granite wheels on Fred's vehicle, Lantieri's crew covered steel drums with fiberglass skins painted to look like granite.

Because it had four more-or-less standard wheels, Barney's car was less complex – although its design had to be revised slightly to translate from drawing to live-action. "In order to put more than one person in Barney's log-shaped car," Levant noted, "it would have had to be really long – which created all kinds of technical problems. So we changed it from a one-log design to a two-log design. From the side, it still looks like Barney's car – so it is very true to the original."

For the obligatory shots of Fred or Barney's feet running beneath their respective cars, Lantieri equipped the vehicles with hand switches that would engage a hidden gas pedal.

"We taught John Goodman and Rick Moranis how to accelerate using the hand switch," Lantieri explained. "They would run, slowly accelerating with their feet; and then, when the car reached some speed, they would pull their feet up and take off. In other shots, where the feet didn't show, they

BELOW: The flashiest of the automobiles was the Le Sabertooth 5000 purchased by Fred when he became a high-roller. INSET: Steel mesh was covered with foam then carved and painted to achieve the Le Sabertooth's sporty look.

could just use the gas pedal. It was fairly simple, but we were concerned about people getting their feet caught underneath the cars and breaking their ankles. We were constantly warning everyone to lift their feet when the cars got going."

Another safety concern with all the cars was their limited braking capacity. Fitted with drum brakes that were less than ideal, the cars could be braked either by hand or pedal, depending upon the angle of a particular shot.

One classically cartoon-like shot in the cars had Fred coming to a sudden stop, with dust and smoke shooting out from his feet. "We prepared the ground with very soft dirt first. Then John came in with the car, jammed his feet down and created a big skid mark in the dirt. We ran air lines down the backs of his legs to blow dust out from the bottom of his feet. It was the kind of cartoon gag we *knew* we'd be doing in this show."

By far the flashiest and most refined of all the vehicles was Fred's sporty Le Sabertooth 5000. In designing the car, director Brian Levant had looked at books featuring classic Corvettes.

"We found grilles that we liked and translated them into bone," Levant said. "I also remembered a car from *Topper* that had a big fin in back – it was like the 1940 Batmobile. So we took all those design features and put them into the Le Sabertooth. We also decided to make it look as if it was made of petrified wood so it would be sleek and polished, yet still organic. "In its final form, the Le Sabertooth was a reddish, round-edged sportscar equipped with the fastest motor, the best suspension and the best steering mechanisms of all the vehicles.

Of all the props and devices made for *The Flintstones*, nothing generated as much excitement

70

as the cars. "Our biggest problem was just keeping everyone off of them," Lantieri commented. "*Everybody* wanted to drive a *Flintstone* car, or have their picture taken in it – and we were just trying to make sure they would make it through to the end of shooting."

The Rock Slicer

Besides the cars, Lantieri's biggest assignment involved the rock slicer – the giant machine that replaces all the quarry workers in the modernization scam promoted by Cliff Vandercave. Art director Nancy Patton had tackled the primary design task for the rock slicer, producing a number of sixteenth-scale models as the concept evolved. Once a design was finalized, the problem of recreating the models in full-scale was turned over to Lantieri.

"The rock slicer was a huge football field-sized machine with all kinds of working hatchets to slice stone, wheels and gears, and a conveyor belt that was about a hundred feet long which moved boulders on carts. The boulders were the size of cars, eight or nine feet in diameter, and they would move in to be sliced into prefab walls for houses. It also had a machine to punch windows inside the

ABOVE: The rock slicer – a huge piece of equipment which featured wheels, gears and conveyor belts – figured prominently in the movie's climax. The crew prepares to shoot a rock slicer scene. LEFT: After Cliff Vandercave straps Pebbles and Bamm-Bamm to the deadly machine, Fred attempts to save the children by bringing the rock slicer to a halt.

ABOVE: Barney tries to save Pebbles and Bamm-Bamm who have been strapped to a cart on the rock slicer conveyor belt. For more dangerous shots in the sequence, dummies were used. ABOVE RIGHT: The crew sets up the shot where Barney is fired from a catapult towards the rock slicer in an attempt to save Pebbles and Bamm-Bamm.

or organic looking reeds. Everything on it was dressed to look like bone or rock or bamboo."

The rock slicer was the setting of the film's climax, in which Pebbles and Bamm-Bamm are strapped to the carts moving through the deadly machine. Obviously, the children's safety was a primary concern in the shooting of the scene. "In a lot of shots, we just pulled the carts by hand, very easily, so there was no chance of the kids getting hurt. Also, Brian shot the scene with long lenses so that it looked as if the kids were much closer to the machine and in much more jeopardy than they really were. We used doubles in some shots, and even Pebbles and Bamm-Bamm dummies."

rock slabs. It was all powered by pneumatics with the motors hidden behind rocks and cables hidden underneath vines

Creatures

In addition to engineering the rock slicer and cars for the movie, Lantieri interfaced closely with the Henson team, providing rigs and mechanical support for the puppets, and rigging sets to accommodate the puppeteers. The special effects team was also crucial to the success of the Henson-built Brontocrane. While the Henson team operated the huge rig, Lantieri's crew was responsible for its forward movement on a track and for its crane transports from one area of the shooting location to another. Similarly, Lantieri was instrumental in realizing the lizard-powered elevator inside the Slate headquarters. While the lizard itself was a Henson puppet, a series of pulleys and cables were rigged by Lantieri to drive the elevator from off-camera. The Henson-Lantieri interface was likewise evident inside the Flintstone house, where Lantieri provided the plumbing and water for the mastodon faucet and shower, as well as rigs to support the Pigasaurus garbage disposal. "The Pigasaurus was a very comical pig with a lot of personality," Lantieri commented, "and it made everyone laugh on the set. There was a scene where Wilma tells Fred that the Pigasaurus is acting up again, and he goes into the kitchen to fix it. He reaches down into its mouth and pulls out a bent spoon, then realizes that his watch is gone.

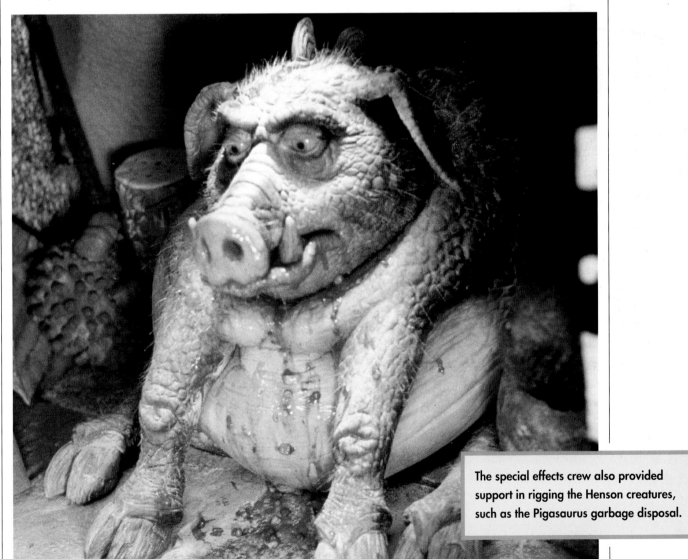

The special effects crew also provided support in rigging the Henson creatures, such as the Pigasaurus garbage disposal.

could make the top of the car bulge and finally pop through. Ultimately, we made a breakaway top in Fred's car, then used a Tupperware tub that was slightly smaller than Dino's head to bulge the top and finally break through the roof. The tub was on a wire attached to a crane overhead and we just tugged on it until it pulled through. It was the right shape for Dino's head, so ILM was able to just animate over it."

Lantieri's crew also created the interaction of Dino on a floor rug for the scene in which the Flintstone pet excitedly greets his master. "Using cables, we made the rug move and curl up under Dino, bunching it up and timing it to what would be the action of Dino's legs once the CG element was in the scene."

Other interactive scenes had Dino moving through his dog door. "It sounds simple but getting the action of the door just right was critical – it had to look as if his nose just bumped it first, and then it had to fly up. So it took a bit of thought to open and close the door properly. What we do on the set really traps the CG team. They have to time their anima-

ABOVE: For the recreation of the cartoon opening – in which Fred slides off the tail off his Bronto-crane and into his waiting car – John Goodman was suspended from a crane supplied by the special effects team. **RIGHT:** The animatronic Dino head pops through the roof of Fred's car in another opening sequence shot. Because the previous shot featured a computer graphic Dino, special effects supervisor Michael Lantieri had to provide the action of Dino's head popping through – an effect he achieved by pulling a tupperware tub through a prescored car top.

So he yells at the Pigasaurus to give it back, and his watch flies up from underneath the sink. For that, we installed a slingshot-like rig under the sink to shoot the watch out."

Another key aspect of Lantieri's *Flintstones* assignment was providing effects that would suggest the interaction on the set of ILM's computer generated (CG) characters. Because the CG characters were obviously not in the set at the time the background plates were shot, effects such as Dino's head popping through the top of Fred's car at the drive-in, or Dino's doggie door opening and closing, had to be achieved with a variety of rigs and wires.

"For the drive-in sequence, Mark Dippe and I watched the cartoon and talked about how we

tion to those actions, and so it is important that we get it right. Mark was always on the set when we shot background plates for the CG. His input was crucial to getting it right from a digital standpoint."

As it had been on *Jurassic Park*, Lantieri's relationship with ILM was a symbiotic one. Through digital wire and rig removals, ILM granted Lantieri greater freedom in setting up his mechanical devices; and by providing interactive gags, Lantieri helped ILM to put their digital characters into scenes more convincingly.

"People always ask me if CG has eliminated my work," Lantieri noted, "but my work has increased as the result of digital technology. I'm hiring more people these days because there is so much interactive stuff that has to be created with computer generated characters to bring them into a real world. We have now become puppeteers in a sense – puppeteers of Tupperware and trees and rugs and vehicles. It takes a puppeteer's sensibility to be aware of characterization and the actions of that character and how it will impact its surroundings. There is a real art to it – it isn't just a matter of violently and artlessly crushing things or moving things around."

Throughout the filming, Lantieri found the experience to be a kind of joyous release from the high pressure and extraordinary demands he had recently faced on *Jurassic Park*. "This movie was kind of the flip side of *Jurassic* – almost a chance to poke fun at the things we'd had to take so seriously on that film. Instead of having to rig a crane that would look *exactly* like a real brachiosaur, we were rigging cartoon-style Bronto-cranes with harnesses and silly control cabs strapped to them. On *The Flintstones*, we got to laugh."

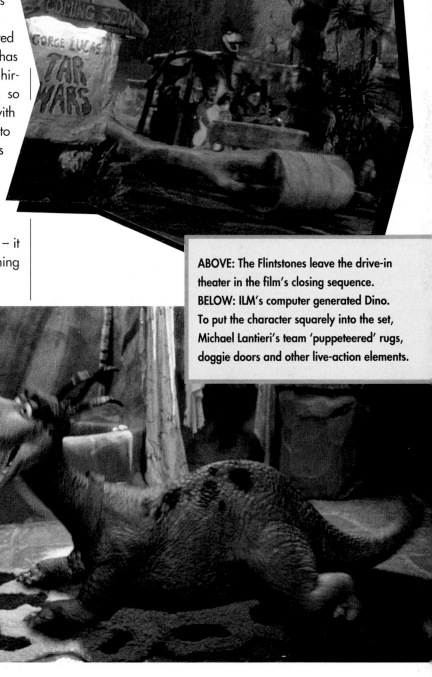

ABOVE: The Flintstones leave the drive-in theater in the film's closing sequence.
BELOW: ILM's computer generated Dino. To put the character squarely into the set, Michael Lantieri's team 'puppeteered' rugs, doggie doors and other live-action elements.

75

CHAPTER 6

"WHEN YOU'RE WITH THE FLINTSTONES..."

THE SHOOT

Filming of *The Flintstones* began on May 17, 1993, on Stage 24 at Universal Studios. For two weeks prior to the start of principal photography, however, Brian Levant and his principal actors had rehearsed, blocking out all but the final scenes of the movie.

"It was a wonderful rehearsal period," Levant recalled. "We decided exactly what we were going to do, rehearsing right in our sets with as many props as we could get, and with the puppets. We figured out everything that was going to happen – which meant that we didn't have to figure it out when we were shooting and there were ninety people standing around looking at their watches."

The rehearsal period also afforded the actors an opportunity to develop their characters, each in his or her own unique way. John Goodman approached the broad, cartoon character of Fred Flintstone just as he would any other role. "Like any part, it was a matter of accepting the setup and then going with it," Goodman said. "I couldn't really go on a tangent playing Fred Flintstone, or give it any

TOP: Cliff Vandercave (Kyle MacLachlan) and Miss Stone (Halle Berry) plot their embezzling scheme from the offices of the Slate & Co headquarters. **ABOVE:** Brian Levant directs MacLachlan prior to shooting a scene at the rock quarry.

rehearsed, because the marks were all set and we couldn't start surprising the audio people and the camera people.

Part of the challenge for Moranis was creating a character whose body shape was quite different from his own – or any other real human being's. In the cartoon, Barney is basically an egg with a head on top of it. "I'm not that round, and I didn't want to do a Robert De Niro trick and put on sixty pounds for this movie; so I relied on padding in my costume to give me a more Barney-like shape. I also played around with my neck and shoulders a little bit, crunching my neck down and bringing my shoulders up. For Barney's voice, I didn't try to copy what Mel Blanc had done, but I couldn't use my own voice either; so I just tried to find that slightly Long Island-ish quality that Barney had."

Strangers before the start of *The Flintstones*, Goodman and Moranis developed a camaraderie and a complementary working style that clicked from the first day of rehearsals and continued throughout the production schedule. "What Rick and John were conscious of from the very beginning," Levant observed, "was that Fred and Barney are a comedy team – the classic big-man/little-man team. When you think of Laurel and Hardy, Abbott and Costello, or Gleason and Carney, you're talking about people who spent *years* together. With John and Rick, in a matter of weeks they went from being 'John and Rick' to 'The Boys.' They became a team; they jelled. They played off of each other and made you believe they had been friends since the age of ten."

A similar kind of camaraderie was developed between Elizabeth Perkins and Rosie O'Donnell, despite the fact that the actresses came from widely different professional backgrounds. Whereas Perkins was a theater-trained dramatic actress, O'Donnell had come from the on-your-feet atmosphere of the comedy clubs. "Between scenes," O'Donnell laughed, "Elizabeth would be studying her lines, looking for Wilma's motivation – and I'd

kind of different interpretation or twist. I had to have the voice down and Fred's basic character – which is a man with a heart of gold who loves his family more than anything else in the world. Mainly, I just tried to find the human relationships – and the cheap laughs."

Rick Moranis relied heavily on his improvisational skills to create the character of Barney. "We improvised a lot during rehearsals," Moranis said, "and also during read-throughs. We were constantly trying to come up with new stuff. Once we were shooting, though, we had to stick to what we'd be sitting there joking with the crew and having a coke. And I'd say to her: 'Honey, it's a *cartoon*! It's not *Sophie's Choice*!'"

"Rosie and I had to adopt a common language because we work so differently," Perkins admitted. "I was probably more serious than I had to be, while she brought a real levity to it. So I think we learned from each other and reached a happy medium. It was important that we work together and develop that common language because in many of their scenes, Wilma and Betty react as a team – they do double takes to each other and things like that. In the beginning, when we had to work some piece of business out, I'd approach her with something Stanislavski-like, and she'd come back with, 'Well, I don't know, I just thought I'd make a geeky face there.' But we learned to play off each other really well. Rosie is the kind of actress you can throw *anything* at in a scene and she will go with it. She is so on top of things in an improvisational way, you can take risks with her you couldn't take with another actor."

One of the first things Perkins focused on in creating Wilma was finding her own version of the voice Jean Vander Pyl had established for the character in the cartoon. "Wilma's voice is very high and a little raspy and very nasal," Perkins commented. "For me, getting the voice down was ninety percent of the role. Jean Vander Pyl told me before we started the movie that the biggest thing to remember in playing Wilma was that the word 'Fred' was always two syllables. It is a little thing, but those are the nuances that people recognize. Nobody wants to come and see a *Flintstones* movie where all the actors have made the characters 'their own.' I felt that the closer we could get to recreating the cartoon, the better audiences would accept it."

While approximating Wilma's vocal quality was a fairly easy task for the actress, Perkins found that much of Wilma's cartoon physicality and body language could not be translated exactly. "She held her hands in a funny way; she walked

> **Fired from the quarry and forced to drift from one demeaning job after another, Barney finally confronts Fred at Cavern on the Green.**

Elizabeth Perkins with Jean Vander Pyl,
the original voice of Wilma.

"The last day of shooting, Rick and I were on the set at Cavern on the Green, and we were supposed to walk out of the club. We'd shot the whole movie, it was our last day, it was about ten-thirty at night, and *all we had to do was walk out.* I don't even remember what got us going, but we burst into a fit of hysterics and we just couldn't stop. We tried to do this last shot four or five times in a row, and every time we'd start laughing. People were starting to get mad because everyone wanted to go home, but we couldn't stop. It took us an hour-and-a-half to walk out of Cavern on the Green . . ."

Rosie O'Donnell

funny. So I had to find physical things that were reminiscent of the cartoon, without looking idiotic. Rosie and I made the decision that Wilma and Betty would always stand with their legs positioned like beauty contestants, for example – which is how they stood in the cartoon. There were little things like that we had to remember to carry through the whole movie."

Rehearsals were well underway when official word came down that Elizabeth Taylor had been signed to play Pearl Slaghoople. Because of Taylor's legendary status, many cast members were more than a bit apprehensive at the prospect of working with her – particularly Elizabeth Perkins, who had sev-

eral scenes with the actress. "The day we found out that she was going to do the movie," Perkins recalled, "I went home and freaked. As an actress, there were certain performances I had always pointed to and said, 'I want to get there someday,' and Elizabeth Taylor's performance in *Who's Afraid of Virginia Woolf?* was one of them. So it was a really big deal for me to be working with her; and I was extremely nervous and intimidated."

O'Donnell had felt some trepidation as well. "What do you say to a living legend – 'Hi, I have your perfume?' She is such a big star, you couldn't help but have reverence for her." Scheduled to shoot on five separate days throughout principal photography, Taylor was greeted on the *Flintstones* set by an entire crew – normally attired in jeans and T-shirts – sporting ties, a dressing room with steps painted her signature shade of violet, and over thirty bouquets of flowers from friends, producers, cast members and studio executives.

Within moments of Taylor's appearance on the set, the actress had managed to put everyone at ease. "When I first met her," John Goodman recalled, "I put on kind of a bull front. She was sitting there with her little dog, and I pointed to the dog and said, 'Lunch.' And she laughed – so I knew she was going to be okay."

"She was completely approachable," Perkins affirmed. "She showed up for rehearsal without a stitch of makeup on, and with her hair pulled back in a bun – and she was still stunning. She was so generous with me, and so kind. I think she knew I was blown away, and she tried to make it easier for me."

While to some *The Flintstones* might have seemed an unlikely vehicle to mark the end of Taylor's fourteen year absence from the big screen, the actress herself did not find the prospect at all unusual. "I've been prepared to do anything in my career," Taylor said, "and ending up being in a cartoon doesn't seem unseemly at all. It seems very fitting! It was great fun, as much fun as I thought it would be."

80

CINEMATOGRAPHER
Dean Cundey

As the actors prepared for the rigorous shooting schedule, cinematographer Dean Cundey attended to the technical demands of the shoot. From the beginning, Bruce Cohen had been convinced that Cundey was indispensable to the movie.

"I didn't know that this movie could be made in the time we had and on the budget we had if we couldn't get Dean Cundey," Cohen stated. "He photographed *Jurassic Park*, *Roger Rabbit* (1988), all three *Back to the Future* movies, *Death Becomes Her* (1992), *Hook* (1991)– he is the master of filming big effects movies, and making them look beautiful and real. On top of that, he has a terrifically dry and wonderful sense of humor; so I knew he and Brian would work well together."

Brian Levant had mandated a lighting and camera style that was bright, funny and happy, and Cundey was responsible for capturing those qualities on film. "The idea of translating an animated subject to live-action was very exciting to me," Cundey stated. "*The Flintstones* required a kind of stylized, heightened reality to it, and I was interested in accomplishing that without making it look odd or hokey."

Although filming was not to begin until the middle of May, Cundey started preparing for the film as early as January, conferring with the art department to determine the overall look of the film. "I also met with Brian early on and talked to him about his vision of the film and any specific images he

BELOW LEFT: The crew prepares to film an establishing shot of suburban Bedrock from a camera crane. BELOW: A veteran of some of the biggest effects films of recent years, cinematographer Dean Cundey was a key member of the *Flintstones'* creative team.

might have in mind. In general, I try to just get a feel for a movie first, instead of going to the script and immediately making extensive notes. Then I start working with the technical crew – the gaffer, the key grip, the camera people – and we decide on the equipment we'll need and how we are going to work out specific problems."

One of the potential pitfalls of *The Flintstones*, from a cinematography standpoint, was the lighting and photography of the Henson puppets. "Shooting puppets and making them look real is one of the most difficult things to do. You have to keep them from being too static in the frame, keep them a little shadowed so you don't see rubber skin, and work with the puppeteers so that you can hide them while

The Henson puppeteers sort out the animation of Dino, Fred's pet, one of the hardest elements of the film to shoot.

still keeping the camera moving and the creature moving. In this case, there was a certain dichotomy with the creatures, because they were caricatures, and as such they weren't *really* supposed to be real. And yet they still had to be believable. The facial expressions had to be logical and they had to look as if they were real, at least within the world of the *Flintstones*."

Principal Photography

Cundey, the actors, Levant and the entire production team were well prepared by the time principal photography commenced. With only thirteen weeks scheduled – twelve for principal photography, and one for second unit work – it was to be an unusually fast-paced shoot.

"It was very important that we not fall behind," Levant explained, "because we had financial constraints and time constraints – we had to get John Goodman back to *Roseanne* by the end of August, and Rosie had another project she was going right

into. So we had a very strict time schedule which meant that we had to shoot two-and-a-half pages a day – and that's pretty fast for a movie. But I'm very comfortable with that kind of pace. I think it helps to make things fresh and spontaneous and not over-rehearsed or over-thought."

Early in the schedule, the production company moved to Vasquez Rocks where they shot for approximately three weeks, filming both day and night exteriors in the suburban neighborhood set.

"Lighting night exteriors in a large area like Vasquez is tricky," Dean Cundey noted. "We were shooting in a very big area with a set that was spread out over two or three blocks, with large rock areas in the background. And it was important that we see those background rocks because that's what we were there for. So we set up Musco lights, which are fairly new exterior lighting units that make night-time shooting easier and faster and more effective."

Among the scenes shot at Vasquez was an opening sequence in which Fred and Barney sing 'The Twitch' as they drive home from work. In a nod to the animated show, the daytime exterior sequence included shots in which the same buildings appeared over and over again in the background as Fred's car drove by.

"When I first told people that I was doing *The Flintstones*," Levant said, "there were always a few who asked if the characters were going to keep going past the same buildings when they drove. So we did that. We had a limited camera track, and when we ran out of road we just went back to the

The crew shoots a night exterior at Vasquez Rocks. To capture the dramatic backgrounds at Vasquez, large Musco lighting units were set up at the location.

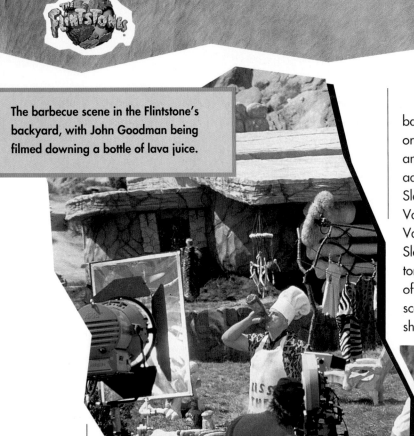

The barbecue scene in the Flintstone's backyard, with John Goodman being filmed downing a bottle of lava juice.

From Vasquez the production company moved back to the sound stages at Universal to shoot interiors of the Slate & Co. headquarters, the Flintstone and Rubble houses, and scenes inside the Bedrock adoption and employment agencies. Included in the Slate interiors were scenes in Fred's office, in Cliff Vandercave's office, and in the boardroom where Vandercave makes his presentation of the proposed Slate Co. modernization. Among the board of directors featured in the scene is Bill Hanna. "I played one of the directors at this huge conference table. In the scene I don't like the modernization idea, so I'm shaking my head and holding my nose and making

beginning again. I don't know if most audience members will notice it – but the kind of people who asked me that question definitely will."

Visible to motorists traveling the Antelope Valley Freeway, the Vasquez Rocks location attracted literally thousands of sightseers during the construction and filming periods. On Memorial Day weekend alone more than thirty thousand people came to see the *Flintstones* neighborhood; and on any given day during the shoot hundreds of visitors were on the set.

"We would have three or four hundred people watching as we were shooting," Bruce Cohen stated. "They would sit on the rocks kind of in rows so it was as if we had a live studio audience. They would laugh at the funny things – and clap when scenes were over. It was great. On a more serious movie it would have been a disaster; but we loved it because it created a really fun atmosphere."

84

faces all through this guy's presentation. Then, at one point, I turn to the president and say, 'He's a madman!' It was my only line."

By the beginning of July, the production company had more or less settled at the quarry in Sun Valley to shoot exterior scenes in downtown Bedrock and at the Slate quarry. The mid-summer heat was amplified in the rocky and tree-less location, making the quarry shoot one of the most difficult periods for both the cast and crew.

"It was pretty uncomfortable," Elizabeth Perkins recalled. "It was hot and I had a two-pound wig on my head, and I was wearing a very tightly corset-

ed leather dress. Sometimes it got to be a hundred and twenty degrees down there. So there were days that went on forever."

"The sun was reflecting off the side of the quarry," Moranis agreed, "literally baking us. And what made it worse was that there was this beautiful lake in the middle of the quarry that we weren't allowed to go in. It was so hot, all you wanted to do was jump in. But we had to pretend it wasn't there. It was like a beautiful mirage."

Involved in some of the film's more complicated action sequences, Moranis spent many of his days at the quarry being dragged, catapulted, shoved down steep hills and hung from giant cranes. The most complicated action sequence was toward the end of the movie when Cliff Vandercave straps Pebbles and Bamm-Bamm to carts moving through the deadly rock slicer machine. In order to save the children in time, Barney ejects himself from a catapult and flies hundreds of feet through the air.

LEFT: After days on location, the production company moved to the soundstages at Universal Studios. In Fred's office, Cliff Vandercave extends a supposedly warm welcome to the new executive. BELOW: Barney strapped to a giant catapult.

"The most important part of doing the physical stuff was meeting my stunt man and seeing that he was indeed the same height and had the same color hair," Moranis joked. "I did do some of it myself, but nothing that was very dangerous. In the rock slicer scene toward the end, where Barney is catapulted into the machine, I got into the catapult and did the beginning of the shot; but it was actually the stunt man who flew through the air. I was also wired up and hung off a crane and swung around, but it was all very safe. The special effects guys were real pros, so I never worried about that stuff."

While principal photography continued at the quarry off and on for nearly two months, days back at the sound stages were interspersed throughout the schedule. Scenes such as Fred's surprise party at the Rubbles' – which featured a cameo by Jean Vander Pyl as Miss Felspar – were completed on the interior sets. The

last sequence to be filmed was a party at Cavern on the Green. Among the 'beautiful people' featured in the blowout scene was Joe Barbera, driving up to the posh club in a fancy, foot-powered car. Featuring the 'BC-52s' singing 'The Twitch,' the entire cast, and hundreds of extras, the Cavern on the Green sequence was a three-day grand finale to the shoot.

ABOVE RIGHT: In the movie's climax, Pebbles and Bamm-Bamm are kidnapped by Vandercave and strapped to a cart moving through the deadly rock slicer machine. **RIGHT:** The film crew prepares to shoot a scene at the CalMat quarry.

It's a Wrap

After a grueling sixty-seven days of principal photography, and a final week of second unit shooting, *The Flintstones* wrapped on August 20, 1993. It had been a shoot characterized by heat, hard work, lightning-quick setups – but mostly, fun and laughter.

"Shooting this movie was the most fun I've ever had," Rick Moranis said. "It was a combination of great people, light and playful material . . . and the fact that we were working for a company that was making billions of dollars on *Jurassic Park*, which meant that we were under no pressure at all."

"It was a situation where you could get up every day knowing you were going to have a fun day at work," John Goodman concurred. "You couldn't really take it too seriously. If I ever started getting too full of myself, all I had to do was look down and see that I was wearing an orange shammy dress with a big blue tie – and that kind of put me in my place."

"Nobody loves the *Flintstones* more than Brian Levant," Eliza-beth Perkins concluded, "and that was the driving force that kept all of us going. There were times when the schedule was tight and when it was over a hundred degrees in the quarry and when my wig felt like it weighed a hundred pounds – but we all sensed that this project meant more to Brian than anything in the world, and so we couldn't let him down by being tired or bitchy. We wanted to give one hundred percent, because he was so enthusiastic."

"Before we started shooting, I went to Brian Levant and said, 'I think Betty and Wilma should have nail polish on. In some of the cartoons you can see that they have nail polish on their hands and toes; and after all, they *are* these well put-together, well mani-cured Fifties' housewives, so they would have their nails done.' And Brian said, 'I have a problem with that . . . I mean, where would they get nail polish?' And I thought, 'Oh, yeah, he's right . . .' So we were standing there, thinking about this, when suddenly it hit me! '*Brian*, we've got satellite dishes! We've got microwave ovens, television sets, *cars*! We've got a whole town with automatic teller machines and gas stations! And you're worried about where the *nail polish* comes from?' And he said, 'Well, you've got a point there . . .'"

Elizabeth Perkins

Mr Slate proclaims Fred a genius as he extols the virtues of Fred's invention 'Concrete' (named after his daughter Concretia).

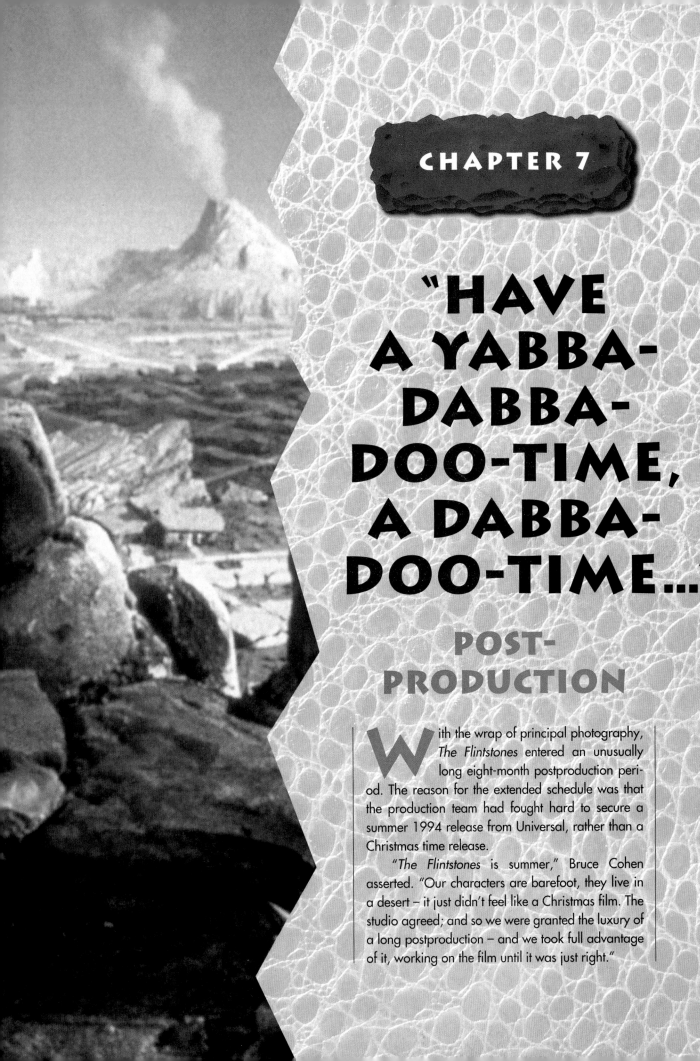

CHAPTER 7

"HAVE A YABBA-DABBA-DOO-TIME, A DABBA-DOO-TIME..."

POST-PRODUCTION

With the wrap of principal photography, *The Flintstones* entered an unusually long eight-month postproduction period. The reason for the extended schedule was that the production team had fought hard to secure a summer 1994 release from Universal, rather than a Christmas time release.

"*The Flintstones* is summer," Bruce Cohen asserted. "Our characters are barefoot, they live in a desert – it just didn't feel like a Christmas film. The studio agreed; and so we were granted the luxury of a long postproduction – and we took full advantage of it, working on the film until it was just right."

The primary tasks of the postproduction phase were the finalizing of ILM's computer generated shots – completed on February 14 – the final editing of the film, and the completion of the sound design and sound mixing.

Editing

Editor Kent Beyda had actually begun the editing process on the first day of filming. "I began right away putting scenes together, and I was really happy with what I was getting. I could see how successful Brian had been in capturing the *Flintstones* world, and the actors had all done a phenomenal job. So, from an editing standpoint, I was real lucky because I had great stuff to work with."

An editor who had worked on Rob Reiner's cult comedy *This Is*

Spinal Tap (1984) early in his career, and had recently edited Billy Crystal's *Mr. Saturday Night* (1992), Beyda understood the careful timings required in a comedy. "You have to preserve the jokes, the elements that made you laugh the first time you saw it. The best comedy directors are the ones that know that the comedy has to play in the master. If the timing is right there in the actor's delivery, then you don't have to go back and try to create it in the editing. Brian definitely had that sense, which made my job a lot easier."

Several weeks after the end of production, Beyda and Levant had a 108-minute rough cut of the film. "After more finessing," Beyda said, "we got it down to 91 minutes – which is a good length for a comedy, especially a comedy that kids were going to want to see. We didn't really cut out anything major – we just condensed what was there."

The editing process also provided Levant with the opportunity to fine-tune the movie. "There were

Fred sees pterodactyls after being clobbered by Barney.

I present him with as finished a work as possible which meant making certain choices early on that normally we would have left until much later. Kent and I were really tough on ourselves so that we could deliver what was essentially a finished film. I was really happy that we were able to just show it to him, turn him into an audience and let him enjoy the movie on that level. Spielberg's enthusiastic response to the film was a huge boost to Levant and the entire production team as they continued to work toward a final cut.

Sound Effects

As the film was being edited and refined, sound designers Mark Mangini and John Pospisil were creating sound effects for everything from a stegosaurus time clock to a Stone Age version of a telephone. "The sound design for this movie was a really unique project," noted Colin Wilson. "It was vital to the show because it was a large part of bringing the characters and that world to life. The important thing was to keep a balance – to come up with sounds that were in the *Flintstones* cartoony vein but still had a certain realism.

little things we changed that, in some cases, made a big difference," Levant recalled. "For example, there was a shot of Fred saying 'Yabba-Dabba-Doo!' where we had lifted John Goodman on a crane so we could get a really high and exaggerated clicking of his heels. But in the first cut we had lost the heel-clicking because we'd gone to a closeup of him. So we changed that to a wider shot and it was a real improvement.

In addition to refining what was already there Levant inserted some additional gags throughout the editing. In the temporary sound dub, for example, the sound designers had provided cartoon-like bird sounds for a scene at Cavern on the Green in which Barney decks Fred. Inspired by the idea, Levant decided to have computer generated pterodactyls – which had already been modeled by ILM – circling Fred's head in classic cartoon style. "It was something we just thought of after-the-fact and luckily we were able to dig up enough money to add it."

Although still missing its final sound mix and many of the computer generated shots by November 1993 the film was complete enough for a screening by Steven Spielberg – a nerve-racking event for Brian Levant.

"From the time we wrapped every bit of my mind and spirit was concerned with getting ready to screen the film for Steven. It was important to me that

ABOVE LEFT: Editor Kent Beyda at work in the editing suite. BELOW: Crew members set up a shot of the Dictabird in action. Although the puppeteers provided the bird's voice on the set, an actor was brought in to redub the character's lines in postproduction.

A large part of the sound assignment was dubbing in dialogue for the verbose Dictabird. Although a Henson puppeteer had read the Dictabird puppet's lines on the set, an actor's voice was dubbed in for a more fully-realized characterization. "We almost never use the original puppeteer's voice," Mark Mangini noted. "In this case not only did we want a more 'character' voice, but the noise created by the animatronic puppet itself ruined the recording on the set. So it had to be replaced."

More challenging for the sound designers was the creation of cartoon-like animal sounds for the wide variety of creatures in the movie. Replicating the well-known yipping sounds made by Dino in the cartoon was particularly difficult.

In order to research the Dino bark, Pospisil and Mangini studied master sound tapes supplied by Hanna-Barbera. "Mel Blanc did Dino in the original show," Mangini said. "The problem was finding someone who could exactly imitate it, because everyone knows Dino's voice and everyone is in love with it." As a backup in case a Dino sound-a-like could not be found, Mangini pulled pieces of Dino's yapping from the original master tapes. "It was hard because when they recorded Dino, they did it in the same sessions with the other characters, so he is often overlapped. I had to find the little pieces where Dino was yapping and no one else was talking, and then string them together to form a little library of sounds. These were recordings made thirty years ago, so there was also some question as to whether or not the fidelity would hold up in a digital six-track release."

For the Bronto-cranes, the sound team combined lion and elephant roars, the sounds of humpback whales, and John Pospisil's voice, electronically processed. "We didn't want anything too realistic for the dinosaurs," Mangini said. "This was a happy movie and a cartoony movie, so the dinosaurs' voices had to be cartoony as well. In *Jurassic Park* they very successfully recreated what a real dinosaur would sound like; but we were going for a more broad, stylized, happy sound."

The stegosaurus time clock featured small camel vocalizations, as well as a classically cartoon-like 'bone crunching' sound for when the animal bites down on the inserted stone time card. "The biting bone sound is one of my favorites," Mangini admit-

TELEVISION LISTINGS

Saturday

3:00pm The Jetstones (Animated)

4:00pm Greatest Sports Legends, featuring Bobby Ore

5:00pm CNN – Cave News Network, continuous news coverage

6:00pm Have Club, Will Travel, starring Richard Bone (Western)

7:00pm All in the Modern Stone Age Family (Comedy)

8:30pm The Rockford Files, (Drama)

9:00pm Murder, She Chiseled (Mystery)

10:00pm David Copper Ore Special (Magic)

92

ted. "It is goofy, but it really says 'cartoon' to me." Mangini was able to lift the sound straight from a library of Hanna-Barbera sound effects. "I was a sound editor at Hanna-Barbera for four years, so I had a large collection of their sound effects. Also, Bruce Cohen gave me a CD collection of their sound effects that had just about everything from the cartoon on it."

In addition to creating vocal characterizations for the creatures, the sound team also dubbed in sounds of the *Flintstones* cars, the bowling alley, the modernized rock slicing machine, and the busy, jangling offices of Slate & Co.

"What was interesting about this project was that we had to fabricate everything from scratch because it all had to sound like it was made of stone or wood when of course it was made of plaster and foam. What made it really difficult was that Brian told us we couldn't use any metal sounds at all. For the rock slicer, which had a lot of gears and wheels, metallic-like squeals would have been very useful, but we didn't have that option. Brian was adamant about the no-metal rule and we had to be really creative to work around that."

"The Flintstones cars required the sounds of heavy stone rolling along the ground, creaky wood frames and flapping hide canvas tops. Part of the challenge was differentiating between the cars. Fred's original car was the equivalent of an old beat-up Ford Valiant while the Le Sabertooth was a very high-powered machine. So we had to come up with the Rolls Royce equivalent of a Stone Age car sound."

By March 4 – the day sound mixing was slated to begin – the sound design team had completed all the redubbing of dialogue and more than forty original sound designs for *The Flintstones*. The final mix included the sound effects, composer David Newman's musical score as well as bits and pieces of music from the original cartoon.

"We had used a lot of the original *Flintstones* music in the temp dub," Brian Levant recalled, "and it fit beautifully. So a couple of those musical bits survived to the final mix. We re-orchestrated them and re-recorded them but we maintained the spirit of the original cartoon music. Again it was a matter of taking from the old and making it new."

AWARDS

Best Picture Nominees:

Stalagmite 17
Sex, Lies and Cave Paintings
The Maltese Pterodactyl
One Flew Over the Dodo's Nest
Crater Vs. Crater

Best Screenplay:

Dances with Raptors
A Fistful of Sand Dollars
Arocknophobia
Across the World in Eighty Days
An Officer and a Cro-Magnon

Best Visual Effects:

1941 B. C.
Poltergeiser
Raiders of the Lost Rock

The stegosaurus time-clock punches a stone time-card at the quarry. A typically cartoon-like bone-crunching sound was dubbed in for the scene.

CHAPTER 8

"WE'LL HAVE A GAY OLD TIME!..."

The Flintstones had its world premiere in New York City on May 21, 1994 as a benefit for the Elizabeth Taylor AIDS Foundation. Less than a week later, on May 27, it opened in theaters throughout the country. Among movie-goers, excitement over *The Flintstones* had been building ever since the first trailer had been unveiled in theaters a full year before the movie was released. Simply conceived, the trailer had merely featured a 'sing-along-with-Mitch' style bouncing boulder moving over the words to the *Flintstones* theme song, ending with John Goodman's expressive 'Yabba-Dabba-Doo!' Even so simple a teaser had elicited hoots, hollers and applause from theater patrons – a reaction that was magnified when more plot-revealing trailers began to make their appearance in the spring of 1994. While no one at Universal wanted to count their brontosaurs before they were hatched, there was still a feeling that, in *The Flintstones*, the studio had a potential 'rockbuster.'

At Amblin, where *The Flintstones* had been a pet project for almost five years, excitement also mounted as the release date neared. No one felt that excitement more than Brian Levant. Emotionally invested in the *Flintstones* since early childhood, Levant's direction of *The Flintstones* was a professional highlight, and a highly personal experience. "This movie drew upon every skill that I've acquired in my life," Levant observed, "and that was very

satisfying. I doubt that I'll ever again find something that challenges me in the same way. Everything that I've ever done or ever been interested in came together in this protect."

The making of *The Flintstones* was not only a lifelong dream come true for the director, it was also a rewarding and creative collaboration between a talented team of producers, designers and technical crafts people. Most of all, it was just plain fun.

"The fun came out of the basic fact that we were doing *The Flintstones*," Bruce Cohen said. "We were putting so much time and energy into this serious business of making a movie, very intense about the hair and lighting and everything, and suddenly it would hit us – 'We're making *The Flintstones*! We're starting cars with our bare feet and wearing leopard-skin dresses and saying 'Yabba-Dabba-Doo!' And we would just burst into hysterics. So much for the serious business of making movies ... "

That spirit of fun was reflected in a final film that was everything Brian Levant, perhaps the most ardent *Flintstones* fan of all time, could have hoped for. "The movie far exceeded my expectations. There is not a single major element from the cartoon show that isn't present in the movie. And it doesn't have a swear word, or an overt act of violence. It is just a wonderful family film that really embraces the spirit of the *Flintstones* cartoon. I watch it, and I have a Yabba-Dabba-Doo time."

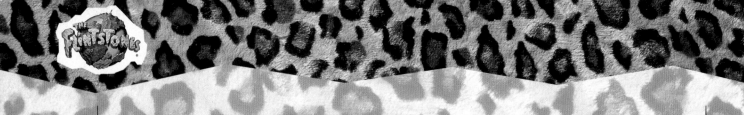

STEVEN SPIELROCK PRESENTS

A Hanna-Barbera/Amblin Entertainment Production
A Brian Levant Film

THE FLINTSTONES ™

**John Goodman
Rick Moranis
Elizabeth Perkins
Rosie O'Donnell
Kyle MacLachlan
Halle Berry
and
Elizabeth Taylor**

MUSIC BY David Newman
COSTUMES DESIGNED BY Rosanna Norton
EDITED BY Kent Beyda, A.C.E.
PRODUCTION DESIGNER William Sandell
DIRECTOR OF PHOTOGRAPHY Dean Cundey, A.S.C.
EXECUTIVE PRODUCERS
William Hanna, Joseph Barbera, Kathleen Kennedy, David Kirschner, Gerald R. Molen
WRITTEN BY Tom Parker & Jim Jennewein and Steven E. deSouza
PRODUCED BY Bruce Cohen
SPECIAL VISUAL EFFECTS BY Industrial Light & Magic
DIRECTED BY Brian Levant